Mike McGrath

Windows 10
Tips, Tricks & Shortcuts

2nd edition
Updated for the Windows 10 Anniversary Update

In easy steps is an imprint of In Easy Steps Limited
16 Hamilton Terrace · Holly Walk · Leamington Spa
Warwickshire · United Kingdom · CV32 4LY
www.ineasysteps.com

Second Edition

In Easy Steps Limited supports The Forest Stewardship Council (FSC),
the leading international forest certification organization. All our titles
that are printed on Greenpeace approved FSC certified paper carry the
FSC logo.

MIX
Paper from
responsible sources
FSC® C020837

Printed and bound in the United Kingdom

ISBN 978-1-84078-748-1

Contents

5   Things You Can Do Without   73

6   Customization   83

7   Paranoia   95

8   Security   107

Installation/Setting Up   123

Shortcuts   137

The Internet   147

Email   167

Multimedia 181

Miscellaneous 195

Index 211

1 Windows 10 Interface

Windows 10 provides a user interface designed for both touchscreen devices and standard screens. Here, we explore its main features.

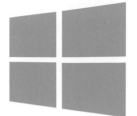

Windows 10 is one operating system with two interfaces – courtesy of **Continuum**.

The **New** icon pictured above indicates a new or enhanced feature introduced in Windows 10 or in the Windows 10 Anniversary Update. For example, the **Continuum** feature is new in Windows 10.

Device Modes

With Windows 10, Microsoft has created an operating system designed to be compatible with a range of different devices. To make this possible, Windows 10 has a new feature called "Continuum" that helps the operating system work better with devices that support both a mouse and keyboard, and touch input. Continuum offers two interface modes for each type of device:

Desktop mode

When a device is in Desktop mode, the layout of the interface is appropriate for mouse and keyboard input. This interface provides a Start menu containing an A-Z list that you can click to launch applications ("apps"). The apps appear in windows, and you can navigate using the mouse buttons or keyboard shortcuts. When you disconnect a mouse and keyboard, or flip your laptop around, you are prompted to change into Tablet mode.

Tablet mode

When a device is in Tablet mode, the layout of the interface is appropriate for touchscreen input. This interface provides a Start screen containing tiles that you can tap to launch apps. The apps appear full-screen, and you can navigate using touch gestures. When you connect a mouse and keyboard, or flip your laptop around, you are prompted to change into Desktop mode.

Tablet mode is less demanding of system resources, and its introduction in Windows 10 clearly indicates that Microsoft considers mobile devices to be where the future lies.

Windows 10 shares its styling and kernel code across multiple devices including smartphones, tablets, PCs and the Xbox console. Also, Windows 10 provides many Universal Windows app programs that are designed for both Desktop and Tablet modes. This move towards cross-device compatibility is one which is intended to firmly establish Microsoft in the mobile market.

A key element in this is the OneDrive app, which enables users to store all their data online and synchronize that data across all their devices. As a result, they will be able to log in to OneDrive on any Windows 10 device and immediately access their data, preference settings, and media, on whatever or whoever's device they are using. So Windows 10 revolves around convergence for all devices, but let's start by taking a look at the various elements that comprise the Windows 10 interface.

Signing in

Lock screen

The first thing you'll see when you start up is the Lock screen, which by default shows the time/date, power, and network status.

The Lock screen is necessary because Windows 10 is a touch-supportive operating system that requires a protective barrier to prevent accidental input. Microsoft has evolved this basic function by enabling users to customize the screen by changing its background and by specifying various notifications to be displayed.

Logon screen

Tap or click anywhere on the Lock screen to reveal the Logon screen, where you can enter your user password or PIN to sign in.

Give your feedback about the **Lock screen** background – if you don't like it, Windows 10 will change it for you.

Although a **Lock screen** is not strictly necessary with a non-touchscreen device, it is a useful place to display information.

Many Windows 10 apps can be configured to display live, real-time data on the **Lock screen**.

Windows Hello has sign-in options for face, fingerprint, or iris – if your device supports these options.

Start Screens

After signing in to a Windows 10 system you will see the Start screen in Desktop or Tablet mode, appropriate for the device:

Start screen in Desktop mode

Click the **Start** button to see the A-Z apps list and pinned tiles appear on the **Start menu** in Desktop mode.

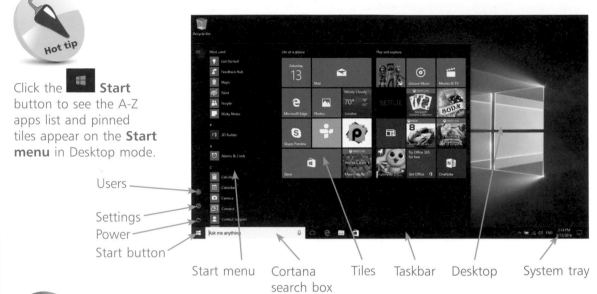

Users

Settings
Power
Start button

Start menu   Cortana   Tiles   Taskbar   Desktop   System tray
              search box

Start screen in Tablet mode

The customizable **Start menu** and Taskbar **Search box** are new features in Windows 10.

In Tablet mode, tap the

All apps button to see the A-Z apps list,

or tap the **Pinned tiles** button to see pinned tiles appear.

All apps   Cortana/Search box   Tiles   Desktop   System tray

In Desktop mode the Start menu contains an A-Z list of apps and pinned tiles – but you switch between these in Tablet mode.

10

Any app in the A-Z list can be added to the pinned tiles by right-clicking on the listed app and choosing **Pin to Start** from the context menu. This allows you to populate the tiles with your favorite apps so you can quickly launch them by clicking, or tapping, on a tile. Apps can also be pinned to the Taskbar in Desktop mode.

The **Search box** lets you easily locate anything you need on your system or on the web. The icons down the side of the open Search box give access to:

- **Cortana** Personal Digital Assistant

- **Home** for news, etc.

- **Notebook** for events, etc.

- **Reminders** for appointments, etc.

- **Feedback** to Microsoft

The **System tray** notification area contains icons that give access to:

- **Battery** status and power settings

- **Network** status and settings

- **Volume** level control

- **Action Center** for notification messages and system settings

- **Clock** date and time settings

- **Show hidden icons** such as "Safely Remove Hardware"

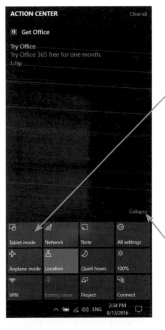

Icons of open or minimized apps appear on the Taskbar. Right-click on the Taskbar to see its options.

Action Center has been completely redesigned to be more easily accessible in Windows 10.

Click the **Tablet mode** button in the **Action Center** to manually switch between Desktop mode and Tablet mode.

Click the **Collapse/ Expand** button in the **Action Center** to hide or show additional configuration options.

11

More Menus

Power User Menu

In Desktop mode, right-click on the Start button, or in Tablet mode, tap and hold the Start button, to open the Power User Menu; a menu of options likely to be of interest to advanced users:

You can also open the **Power User Menu** by pressing **WinKey + X**.

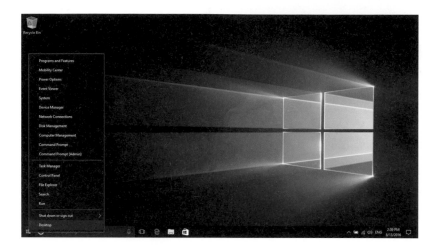

Task View

Click or tap the Task View button to reveal a thumbnail of each open app on the Start screen:

You can also open the **Task View** by pressing **WinKey + Tab**.

Windows' **Task List** can also be used to show open apps by holding down the **Alt** key then pressing the **Tab** key.

Tap or click to select the app you want to work with, or press **WinKey + Tab** again to close Task View.

Navigation

In its drive for Windows 10 to be all-encompassing, Microsoft has made it possible to navigate the interface in three different ways: by touch, the mouse, and the keyboard.

Touch

Touch gestures include swiping, sliding, tapping, and pinching. The best way to get to grips with these is to experiment. The following, however, will get you off to a good start:

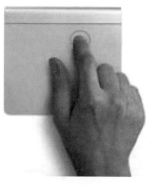

Tap – opens, selects or activates whatever you tap (similar to clicking with a mouse).

Tap and hold – shows further information about the item or opens a context menu (similar to right-clicking with a mouse).

Pinch or stretch – visually zooms in or out, like on a website, map or picture.

Rotate – some items can be rotated by placing your fingers on them and turning your hand.

Slide to scroll – dragging your finger across the screen scrolls through the items (similar to scrolling a mouse wheel).

Slide to arrange – dragging an item around the screen with your finger to position it (similar to dragging with a mouse).

Swipe to select – a short, quick movement will select an item and often bring up app commands.

Swipe or slide from right edge – opens the Action Center.

Swipe or slide from left edge – opens the Task View feature.

Swipe or slide from top edge – enables you to view the Title bar in full-screen apps.

Swipe or slide from bottom edge – enables you to view the Taskbar in full-screen apps.

In many cases, the touch commands available are dependent on the application in use. For example, various rotational commands can be used to manipulate objects in drawing and layout applications such as Microsoft PowerPoint.

Spinning the mouse wheel while on the **Lock screen** will open the **Logon screen**. When on the **Start screen**, it scrolls the app window.

In previous versions of Windows, **WinKey + Tab** opened "App Switcher" – which has now become **Task View**.

The **Alt + Tab** shortcut dates back decades but was retroactively named "Windows Flip" in Windows Vista – it has now become **Task List**.

...cont'd

Mouse

Using the mouse to get around in Windows 10 is no different to any other operating system. The trick is knowing where to position the mouse to reveal the menus and features provided by the interface. See pages 10-12.

Keyboard

Those of you who use the Start screen without the benefit of a touchscreen are well advised to get acquainted with the various keyboard commands relevant to it. In many cases, just as with keyboard commands and shortcuts in general, they are often quicker than using the mouse.

There are actually a whole bunch of these commands, and a full list is shown on pages 144-146. The following are some of the more useful ones:

The most important key is the Windows key, also called WinKey – see page 146. Pressing this key instantly opens the Start screen menu regardless of where the user is. It can also be used in conjunction with other keys to perform other actions. For example, **WinKey + X** opens the **Power User Menu** as mentioned on page 12, while **WinKey + C** opens the Taskbar **Search box**.

The **Home** and **End** keys jump from one end of the Start menu **All apps** A-Z list to the other, while the arrow keys can be used to select a tile. The **Enter** key opens an app.

WinKey + Tab opens the **Task View** list that allows the user to switch to a different app – by scrolling through thumbnails using the arrow keys, then pressing the **Enter** key to select an open app.

Holding down the **Alt** key then pressing **Tab** opens a horizontal **Task List**. You can move between thumbnails by pressing **Tab** then release **Alt** to open the selected app. Note you must have at least two apps running for **WinKey + Tab** and **Alt + Tab** to work.

A rarely-used key known as the **Context Menu** key (usually located close to the space bar) brings up a menu of related options when pressed in an open app. The context menu typically appears at the top of the app window.

Organization

App tiles on the right of the Start menu are larger than the listed items in the A-Z apps list. The more congested the Start menu becomes, the more scrolling is needed to find a particular app.

Organizing Start screen tiles

So, perhaps one of the first things a user new to Windows 10 will do is to introduce some organization into how the Start menu tiles are presented. The most important thing is to place your most frequently accessed apps at the top of the Start menu tiles, where they will be on view by default. Create an app tile by right-clicking on the app and selecting Pin to Start, and then move it by left-clicking and holding on the tile, dragging it to where you want it and then releasing it.

Create and organize groups

The method described above is, however, a laborious way of moving large numbers of app tiles. The solution is to place your app tiles in groups, which can be moved around the Start menu in blocks. This makes it easier to arrange your Start menu, and having your apps in specific related groups makes it much easier to find a particular app. So how's it done? Drag a tile to an empty part of the Start menu, then release it and position the cursor above the top edge of the tile to see a "Name group" item appear there on a group bar. Click this item to make it editable and type a suitable name to create a new group. Take a tile and drag it across the Start menu to see the other tiles move to accommodate that tile within the group (as shown below). Similarly, if you take a group bar and drag it across the Start menu you'll see other groups move to accommodate that group.

An important aspect of organizing the Start menu is placing app tiles in related groups.

The customizable Start menu is a great new feature in Windows 10.

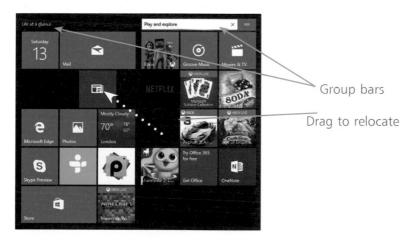

Group bars

Drag to relocate

You can also reduce the size of the large tiles to create more space on the Start menu, which reduces the amount of scrolling necessary. Just right-click on a tile, select **Resize** and choose from the available options.

Universal Windows apps are developed for use across desktop PC, laptop notebook, tablet, and phone devices.

Unless explicitly closed by the user, Windows 10 apps are always open – but, unlike with previous Windows versions, this has a negligible effect on system performance.

It is possible to install third-party apps on Windows 10 – see page 67.

Apps

In keeping with Microsoft's intention of making inroads into the mobile market, the Universal Windows apps created for Windows 10 are designed for both desktop, mobile and tablet screens.

Many of these apps display content in real time. For example, there is a **Weather** app that shows a constantly-updated 10-day forecast and a **News** app that displays current stories and images.

These apps are user friendly and simple. As with the Windows 10 interface itself, Microsoft has designed the apps to be clean and straightforward with the minimum of extraneous clutter – the app's content is intended to dominate. A consequence of this is that the traditional navigational aids such as toolbars, menus, and preview panes, are in evidence to a much lesser degree.

To use Microsoft terminology, the Universal Windows apps are "immersive applications" – which basically means they run best in full-screen mode. For users with a large, wide-screen monitor this is definitely a restriction. However, this is mitigated to a certain extent by a feature called **Snap**. This makes it possible to have up to four apps running side-by-side – we explain how to set this up on page 69.

Traditional Windows programs, such as **Notepad**, will still work in Windows 10. These will appear in their own window when run in Desktop mode but will appear full-screen when run in Tablet mode. It's important to be aware that Universal Windows apps are different to their traditional Windows equivalents.

Sourcing and installing apps

In order to provide as secure a computing environment as possible, official Windows 10 apps are only available from the Windows Store. This effectively "sandboxes" them and, as a result, users are much less likely to introduce viruses and malware to their computers via downloaded software.

To access the Windows Store, click the **Store** tile on the Start screen. You will then be asked to sign in with your Microsoft Account.

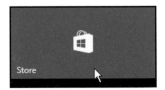

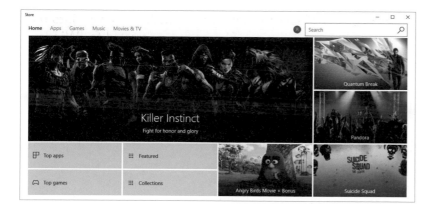

The **Windows Store** may hold less content than other app stores, but it is growing rapidly – check back here often.

The first things you see on the **Home** screen are promoted apps and four category buttons for **Top Apps**, **Featured**, **Top games**, and **Collections**. Below this is a section for **Study and play** apps. This is followed by a **Picks for you** section, which shows a number of apps of the type often used by the user. For example, if you play a lot of card games, this section will feature card game apps. Moving down, there are sections showing **Most popular**, **Top free apps**, **Top free games**, **New music**, **New movies**, **Top-selling TV shows**, and **Collections**.

Selecting any "Top..." category in the Store provides a filter to refine your search.

17

At the top of the window is a menu for **Home**, **Apps**, **Games**, **Music**, **Movie & TV** screens, and a Search box that can locate an app by keyword. Using the sections, screens or search, takes you to the app's page where there are typically

Screenshots, a **Features** description, **Additional information**, and **Ratings and reviews**. Below the app's title is an install button labeled "Free" or with the purchase price. Once you've chosen an app, and paid if required, click the install button to download the app and see it appear on the Start menu's A-Z list.

Check out its **Ratings and reviews** before choosing an app.

By using the same Microsoft Account, all official apps installed on your PC will also be available on any other Windows 10 devices you may have.

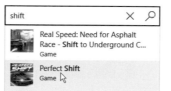

18

Don't forget

Windows 10 minimizes system resource usage – so a whole bunch of apps can be open at the same time without significant performance loss.

Hot tip

If your Taskbar and Desktop disappear unexpectedly, Windows Explorer may have crashed. Press **Ctrl + Shift + Esc**, to open **Task Manager**, then click **File**, **New Task** and type **Explorer.exe** – then click **OK** to restart Windows Explorer.

Hot tip

You can also use **Task Manager** to troubleshoot startup problems and identify memory-hogging apps.

…cont'd

Closing apps

Closing an app is very simple to do, but it must be pointed out that usually it is not actually necessary to close apps. This is because when a new app is opened, other running apps are switched to a state of suspension in which they use very little in the way of system resources.

However, there may be situations in which it is desirable or even necessary to close down an app. Here are five ways to do this:

- Simply press **Alt + F4** – this kills the app instantly.

- Click or tap the **X** (Close) button on the app window's Title bar.

- Right-click the app in **Task View** and select **Close**.

- Hover over the app icon on the Taskbar and select **Close window** in the pop-up context menu that appears.

- Press **Ctrl + Shift + Esc**, to open the **Task Manager**, then right-click to select the app and click the **End task** option.

2 Performance

Windows operating systems require a powerful computer in order to function at their best. Those of you whose systems are struggling to run Windows 10 will be able to achieve a higher level of performance by implementing the measures described in this chapter. We also explain some more general performance-boosting steps that apply to all versions of Windows.

Overview

Operating systems, no matter how good they may be, are completely reliant on the hardware used to run them. If the hardware is not up to the job, while the operating system may function, it will not do so at its best.

If your PC can run Windows 7 or Windows 8.1, it will run Windows 10 just fine.

Even where the hardware is good enough, if it is configured or installed incorrectly, the operating system will be adversely affected. On a slightly different tack, it is often possible to squeeze a bit more performance from a hardware device by tweaking its settings.

In this chapter, we look at these issues and show how to get both your computer and operating system running at their maximum performance level.

Your hardware is the place to start, and the good news is that Windows 10 does not require anything out of the ordinary in this respect. If your computer can run either Windows 7 or Windows 8.1, it will also run Windows 10 without the need for any upgrading.

Hot tip

Even if your PC is running Windows Vista it will run Windows 10, as long as it has the correct specifications.

However, if you do experience any problems, or would simply like to get your computer running as well as possible, there are quite a few adjustments that can be made to the default settings, which will make it run considerably faster. For users whose hardware provides a performance level that is on the borderline between poor and acceptable, these can negate the need for a hardware upgrade.

If your system struggles with Windows 10, there are steps you can take to reduce the demands made by it.

There are also some more general steps that users can take in order to keep their system running, not just at peak performance but also reliably. These are not specific to Windows 10 – they apply to any operating system.

This chapter shows the tweaks that can be made to Windows 10 default settings to improve its performance, and also shows, generally, how to keep your PC running smoothly and reliably.

Please note that in this book, unless otherwise mentioned, we are concentrating on the Windows Desktop mode interface, as is used on traditional mouse controlled desktop PCs, rather than the Windows 10 Tablet mode interface, which is really only suitable for handheld devices and touchscreen monitors.

Add More Memory

Without doubt, the quickest and most effective method of improving the overall performance of any computer is to simply increase the amount of its Random Access Memory (RAM). Windows 10 will not function well with any less than 1GB of memory. Optimum performance will require 2GB.

Adding memory is a simple procedure that takes no more than a few minutes, but does require the system case to be opened. On a PC this reveals the motherboard containing the memory modules:

Open the retaining clips at the ends of an empty memory socket, then insert a new memory module by gently pressing down on the top edge until the clips close automatically.

On a laptop computer you can find an access panel on the underside of the case that reveals the memory modules. Push apart the retaining clips until the socket pops up.

If one or more of the sockets are empty, all you have to do is fit extra modules to complement the existing ones. If the sockets are all in use, you will have to remove some, or all, of the modules and replace them with modules of a larger capacity.

However, if the prospect of meddling inside the case doesn't appeal to you there is an easier, although less effective, option available called **ReadyBoost**, which is explained on page 22.

To discover how much memory your PC has, press **WinKey + R** then type "msinfo32" into the Run box to open the **System Information Summary**, and then scroll down to the **Total Physical Memory** item.

You cannot install just any memory – it has to be compatible. Consult your PC's manual to see which type you need.

Memory modules must be handled very carefully. Before touching one, ground yourself by touching the metal case chassis. If you don't, the electrostatic charge in your body could well damage the module.

Quick Speed Boost

If Windows were to run out of memory, the system would grind to a halt. To prevent this, it uses a "paging file" on the hard drive as a memory substitute. The problem with this is that hard drives are much slower than memory, so performance is reduced when the paging file is being used.

The solution is to prevent Windows having to use the paging file, and the way to do this is to install more memory. However, many users don't know how to install memory – plus, it is expensive.

ReadyBoost provides an easier and cheaper alternative – you just need a USB flash drive with a capacity between 256MB and 4GB.

 Connect the USB drive then right-click its icon in **File Explorer** and select **Properties** from the context menu

 In the **Properties** dialog, choose the **ReadyBoost** tab

 Now, select **Dedicate this device to ReadyBoost**

Click **OK** to create a ReadyBoost cache file in the USB drive

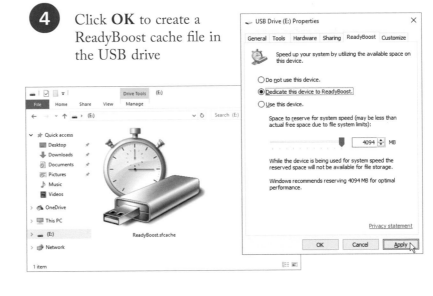

Windows will now use the USB drive as a cache for the most commonly-paged data. The paging file will still be on the hard drive but will be used much less.

Users with less than 1GB of physical memory will benefit the most from using ReadyBoost.

Reduce the Visual Effects

Windows comes with a number of visual effects such as fading or sliding menus, drop shadows, and pointer shadows. These are all designed to improve the look and feel of the Windows interface.

They do, however, add nothing to its functionality. In fact, they can, and do, have a negative impact on the system. Remember that each of these effects consumes system resources.

Users interested in performance rather than appearance will benefit from disabling some, or even all, of these essentially unnecessary graphic enhancements:

 Press **WinKey + X**, to open the Power User Menu, then click **Control Panel** > **System** > **Advanced system settings**

 Next, click the **Settings** button under **Performance**

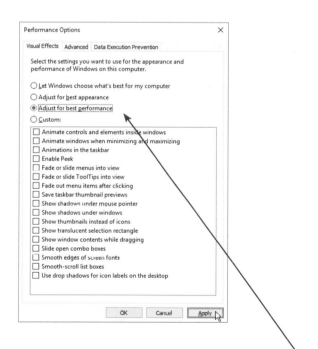

 Now, check the **Adjust for best performance** option

By default, Windows chooses the first option, **Let Windows choose what's best for my computer**, which enables the majority of the effects. You can disable them all as shown above. Alternatively, you can disable them individually.

Windows visual effects are purely cosmetic and serve no practical purpose. Disabling them will have no effect on the PC's functionality.

23

Disabling all effects will have a significant impact on the appearance of the Windows Desktop mode interface.

Adjust for best performance turns off all visual effects. The most common effects to turn off individually are:
Animate controls...
Animate windows...
Fade or slide...
Fade out...
Show shadows...
Slide open...

Icon Thumbnails

By default, Windows displays all file icons as thumbnails (mini graphical representations). This is particularly useful when viewing image files, as it enables you to see the image without having to first open it in an imaging program as shown below:

Graphic files are the slowest file type to load – thumbnails are small but their negative effect on system performance is cumulative.

The **File Explorer Options** item in the Control Panel was previously known as **Folder Options** in earlier versions of Windows.

Check the option shown here to **Show hidden files, folders, and drives** to ensure **File Explorer** provides a comprehensive view of your system contents.

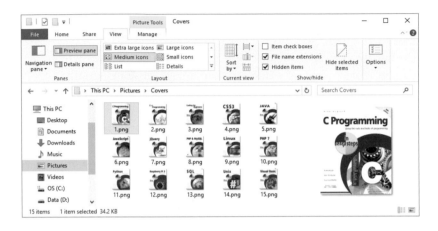

However, there is a downside. Because graphic files take longer to open than any other type of file, having this feature enabled does adversely affect system performance. Users who want their system to run as fast as possible, and those who simply need a performance boost, will benefit by disabling this feature. Do it as described below:

1 Go to **Control Panel** > **File Explorer Options**, then click the **View** tab

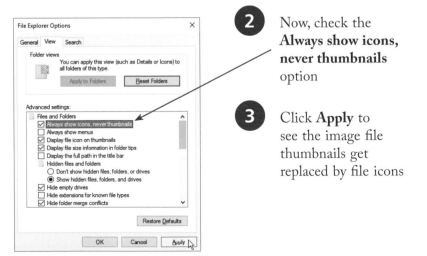

2 Now, check the **Always show icons, never thumbnails** option

3 Click **Apply** to see the image file thumbnails get replaced by file icons

Faster Paging

When Windows runs out of physical memory it uses a special file on the hard drive as a substitute, known as the paging file. Moving it to a different drive speeds up the paging operation, and thus system performance (see first Hot tip). To carry out this procedure you will, of course, need two hard drives:

1 Go to **Control Panel** > **System**, then click the **System protection** link and choose the **Advanced** tab

2 Click **Settings** (under **Performance**) and then the **Advanced** tab. Under **Virtual Memory**, click **Change**

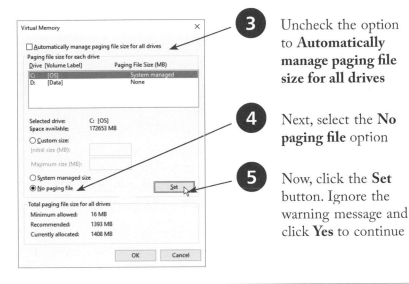

3 Uncheck the option to **Automatically manage paging file size for all drives**

4 Next, select the **No paging file** option

5 Now, click the **Set** button. Ignore the warning message and click **Yes** to continue

6 Select a different drive

7 Select **System managed size**

8 Click **Set** and then click **OK**. Reboot your computer to apply the change

A separate drive that doesn't have Windows and other applications installed on it will be more responsive as it has used much less space than the main drive. So, placing the paging file on it will improve the speed of the paging operation.

The **Custom size** option lets you choose an initial size and maximum size for the paging file.

There is no benefit to be gained by moving the paging file to a different partition on the same drive. It must be moved to a separate drive.

25

Disable Superfetch

The **Superfetch** feature in Windows helps to keep the computer consistently responsive to your programs, by making better use of the computer's memory.

Superfetch prioritizes the programs you're currently using over background tasks, and also adapts to the way you work by tracking the programs you use most often and preloading these into memory. As a result, they open much more quickly when accessed.

On PCs that have 2GB or more of memory, **Superfetch** works very well. However, if your PC has less than 2GB it can lead to excessive disk thrashing (see first Hot tip) and sluggish system performance. The less memory you have, the worse the effect.

If you find yourself in this position, you have three options:

● Upgrade your memory so you have at least 2GB

● Enable **ReadyBoost** – see page 22

● Disable the **Superfetch** feature

The latter is done as follows:

 Go to **Control Panel** > **Administrative Tools**. Double-click **Services** and scroll down to the **Superfetch** service

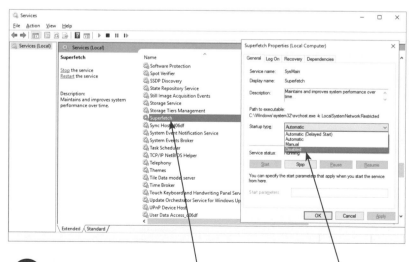

 Double-click **Superfetch**, to open its **Properties** dialog, and in the **Startup type** drop-down box select **Disabled**

Disk thrashing occurs on PCs that are low on memory, which causes the operating system to frequently utilize the hard drive as a memory substitute. This leads to data being constantly transferred between hard drive and memory.

Disk thrashing can damage or cause premature failure of the hard drive due to excessive wear and tear on the read/write heads.

Systems with solid state drives (SSD) may see little, if any, advantage with Superfetch – due to their performance advantage over regular hard disk drives (HDD).

Cancel Unneeded Services

When a Windows PC is being used, in the background and unseen by the user, a number of applications known as **Services** will be running. While many of them are essential for certain functions of the operating system, there are some that are not.

As every running application makes a hit on system performance, this is something you will want to prevent. Fortunately, you can override Windows and make the decision yourself as to which **Services** should be running. As a guide, those **Services** specified in the list on the right can be disabled safely. The procedure for doing so is exactly the same as described on the previous page (Disable **Superfetch**).

However, should you consider disabling any **Services** that are not listed on the right, we suggest that you first take a look at what the service does and also what other applications may be depending on it. Do this as follows:

1 Open the service's **Properties** dialog box, where you will see a description of the service's function

2 Click the **Dependencies** tab to see what other applications depend on this service

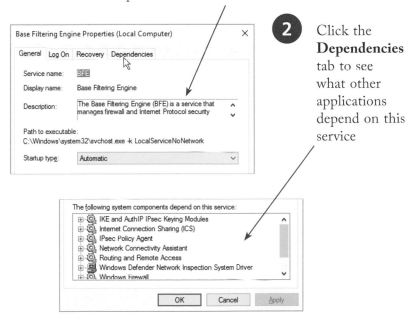

By checking this out, you will not inadvertently disable a service that is essential to the running of your PC.

Hot tip

Services that can be safely disabled are:

- **IKE and AuthIP IPsec Keying Modules**
- **Remote Registry**
- **UPnP Device Host**
- **WebClient**
- **Windows Error Reporting Service**
- **Windows Image Acquisition (WIA)**

If you don't use your PC for networking, the following **Services** can also be disabled:

- **Computer Browser**
- **Distributed Link Tracking Client**
- **Netlogon**
- **Peer Name Resolution Protocol**
- **Peer Networking Identity Manager**
- **SSDP Discovery**
- **Server**
- **TCP/IP NetBIOS Helper**
- **Workstation**

More Shutdown Options

There are several ways to access a Windows 10 PC's power off options. You can do so by clicking the **Start** button then **Power**, by right-clicking the **Start** button, then **Shut down or sign out**, or by clicking the ⏻ Power button on the **Lock screen**.

Here is another way that provides **Shut down**, **Switch user**, **Sign out**, **Sleep**, and **Restart** options. Do it as follows:

This example creates a handy Shutdown script using the **Visual Basic** scripting language called "VBScript".

Shutdown.vbs

Windows 10 includes the **Windows Script Host (WSH)** to provide scripting abilities for the VBScript and JavaScript scripting languages.

You can drag your new **Shutdown** icon to the Taskbar where it can be quickly accessed.

1 Type "notepad" into the Taskbar **Search box** then hit **Enter** – to open the Windows Notepad application

2 In **Notepad**, precisely type the following:
```
dim objShell
set objShell = CreateObject("shell.application")
objShell.ShutdownWindows
set objShell = nothing
```

3 From the file menu, click **Save As** and in the box enter a suitable name, e.g. "Shutdown". Give it the **.vbs** file extension as shown below and save it to the Desktop

4 Double-click the **Shutdown** icon that now appears on the Desktop, to see a **Shut Down Windows** dialog box offering Windows 10 power off options:

Streamline the Registry

The Registry is a central hierarchical database that holds all of the important Windows settings regarding software, hardware and system configuration. It also provides a common location for all applications to save their launching parameters and data.

Over time, as the user installs and deletes programs, creates shortcuts and changes system settings etc., obsolete and invalid key information builds up in the Registry. While this does not have a major impact on a PC's performance, it can be the cause of system and program errors that can lead to instability issues.

The solution is to scan the Registry periodically with a suitable application that will locate all the invalid entries and delete them.

While Windows Registry Editor is adequate for editing purposes, it does not provide a cleaning option. However, there are many of these utilities available for download from the internet. A typical example is **CCleaner** (shown below). These programs provide various options, such as full or selective scans, backups, and the creation of System Restore points.

A free version of the **CCleaner** utility can be downloaded from piriform.com/ccleaner

The **CCleaner** utility can also be used to clean out accumulated junk, such as temporary files, to keep your system running well.

Changes to the Registry can be dangerous, so create a System Restore point using the System Restore utility first – see page 208. If you have any problems as a result of the change, you will be able to undo it by restoring the system to that point.

Occasional use of a Registry cleaner helps keep your system stable and reliable. CCleaner also provides active monitoring to notify you when your system would benefit from a clean.

Optimize the Hard Drive

Hot tip

The ideal way to use an SSD is to set it up as the boot drive and use a cheaper mechanical hard drive for data storage.

Don't forget

Windows 10 provides **TRIM** support that automatically cleans your SSD – to ensure its performance does not degrade with use.

Hot tip

Most SSD manufacturers offer free tools to manage and optimize their solid state drives, such as the **Intel SSD Toolbox**. Check out the manufacturer's website of your own SSD.

Assuming you're not already using one, a very good way of improving not only drive performance but that of the whole PC, is to replace the boot hard drive (the one Windows is installed on) with a solid state drive (SSD).

Replacing the boot hard drive will mean opening up the system case, which is something many users will not be comfortable with. However, if you are prepared to do it, or know someone

who can do it for you, the benefits are considerable. The main one is speed – the "seek" time of an SSD (the time it takes to locate a file) is in the order of .01 ms compared to around 7 ms for a traditional mechanical hard drive. The result is a computer in which boot times, typically, are halved and programs open instantaneously.

SSDs are also far more reliable than mechanical drives as they contain no moving parts. This means it is much safer to store data on an SSD. Other advantages include their small dimensions, low power requirements, and no need for maintenance (defragmentation).

The only real drawbacks of these devices is the cost – two to three times as much as a mechanical drive, and relatively low storage capacity. For these reasons, the use of SSDs is usually restricted to the boot drive, with a mechanical drive providing much larger and cheaper data storage capacity.

Installing an SSD is actually a very simple operation. All that is required is to secure the device in place, then connect the data and power cables to the drive. You'll also need to install a clean copy of the operating system on the drive, or copy it from the existing drive. Full installation and set up instructions are usually supplied with the devices.

Keep it lean and mean

When approximately 70% of a hard drive's storage capacity has been used, its performance level will start to decrease. It will also be more likely to be affected by the issue of fragmentation.

So, when it begins to approach this mark, you should start thinking about freeing up some space. As it's a sure fact that many of the files on your drive will be redundant, you can usually do this without losing anything important:

1 Go to **Control Panel** > **Administrative Tools** then click the **Disk Cleanup** item to scan the file system

2 Under **Files to delete** you will see a list of all the files that can be safely deleted. Check all the boxes and then click **OK** to delete them

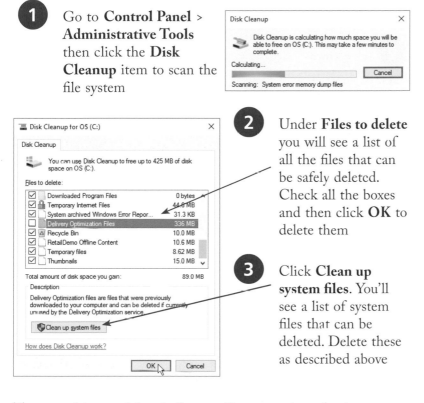

3 Click **Clean up system files**. You'll see a list of system files that can be deleted. Delete these as described above

The next thing to delete is **System Restore** points. As these are actually system backups, they are very large files, often several GBs in size, and there may be several of them. Click **Clean up system files**, then select the **More Options** tab and click **Clean up** under **System Restore and Shadow Copies**.

Finally, click **Clean up** under **Programs and Features**. You'll see a list of all the programs installed on the PC. Go through the list and uninstall any that you don't use. You'll now have even more free disk space.

Beware

The more data you have on your drive, the worse the effects of fragmentation.

NEW

Windows Update Delivery Optimization is new in Windows 10. It helps you get updates more quickly and sends updates to other PCs on your network. Although the Delivery Optimization files are sizeable, you may not want to delete them – see page 116.

Don't forget

System Restore points are created whenever major changes are made to the system. These points can occupy a tremendous amount of disk space, so deleting them is worth doing. The actions on the left delete all but the most recent restore point.

...cont'd

Keep the File System healthy

Over time, especially if the PC is well-used, file system and data faults can build up on the hard drive. Not only can these have an adverse effect on the PC's performance, they can also be the cause of general system instability, and thus potential loss of data.

To correct these types of faults, Windows provides a disk maintenance utility called **Chkdsk**. Access it as follows:

 Press **WinKey + X** to open the Power User Menu. Select **File Explorer**, then choose **This PC**

 Right-click the drive you want to check, and select **Properties**. In the dialog that opens, click the **Tools** tab

Run **Chkdsk** after every incorrect shutdown or system crash. These are the actions that will introduce file system errors to the hard drive. If you don't do this, one day your system may simply refuse to boot up.

Windows 10's version of **Chkdsk** will usually alert the user automatically when it needs to be run.

3 Under **Error checking**, click the **Check** button to open the **Error Checking** dialog

4 In the **Error Checking** dialog box, click **Scan drive**. If **Chkdsk** finds any errors on your hard drive it will attempt to repair them

OS (C:) Properties

Security | Previous Versions | Quota
General | Tools | Hardware | Sharing

Error checking

This option will check the drive for file system errors.

🛡Check

Optimize and defragment drive

Optimizing your computer's drives can help it run more efficiently.

Optimize

OK | Cancel | Apply

You can also type the **Chkdsk** command at an Administrator Command Prompt to scan a drive for errors (right-click **Start**, then click **Command Prompt (Admin)**).

Error Checking (OS (C:))

You don't need to scan this drive

We haven't found any errors on this drive. You can still scan the drive for errors if you want.

→ Scan drive
You can keep using the drive during the scan. If errors are found, you can decide if you want to fix them.

Cancel

Completion reports "**Your drive was successfully scanned**".

Hard drive speed boost

This tip shows how to boost hard drive speed, and thus system performance, by implementing a hard drive configuration technology known as Redundant Array of Independent Disks (**RAID**). This is a way of configuring a combination of hard drives to gain specific benefits; in this case, an increase in drive speed.

To set up a **RAID** configuration, you will need two hard drives and a RAID controller. With regard to the latter, some modern motherboards provide one. Check your motherboard documentation to see if yours does – if so, you're all set. If it doesn't, you'll need to buy a RAID controller PCI card, which you install in a PCI slot on the motherboard.

When you have installed the second hard drive, boot the PC and then press the key specified in the motherboard documentation to open the **RAID** utility.

Hot tip

RAID 0 configuration splits the data across the drives. As each drive handles half the work load, data transfer rates are much improved. However, if either of the drives fail, all of the PC's data will be lost.

RAID 1 configuration copies data to each drive. If one drive fails, the data is recoverable from the other one, but the capacity of one of the drives is lost.

RAID SPAN is merely a way of combining two drives into one – there's no real benefit from it.

```
       VIA Tech. VT8237 Series SATA RAID BIOS Ver x.xx

  ▸  RAID 0 for performance          Create a RAID array with
  ▸  RAID 1 for data protection      the hard disks attached to
  ▸  RAID SPAN for capacity          VIA RAID controller
  ▸
                                     F1    : View Array/Disk Status
                                     ↑,↓   : Move to next item
                                     Enter : Confirm the selection
                                     ESC   : Exit


    Channel         Drive Name     Array Name Mode  Size(GB) Status

  Serial_Ch0 Master XXXXXXXXXXX    ARRAY 0   SATA   999.99   XXXXXXX

  Serial_Ch1 Master XXXXXXXXXXX    ARRAY 0   SATA   999.99   XXXXXXX
```

Typically, you will be given three options: **RAID 0, RAID 1**, and **RAID SPAN**. Most **RAID** setup utilities offer an auto-setup option. All you have to do is specify the configuration required, which in this case is **RAID 0**. The utility will then set up the configuration automatically; the process taking only a few seconds. Reboot and you're done. Go to **This PC** and you will see just one drive, but with the combined capacities of the two drives.

Update Device Drivers

What exactly is a driver? Well, let's assume that you are about to print a document and have opened your printer software to change a few settings. What you are looking at is actually a driver, in this case your printer's driver. A driver has three purposes:

- First, some drivers, like the printer driver mentioned above, act as an interface between the device and the user – allowing changes to be made to the way the device operates.

- Second, all drivers act as an interface between their device and the operating system. They tell the operating system what system resources the device needs for correct operation.

- Third, drivers provide a way for hardware manufacturers to update their devices to take account of advances in technology, both hardware and software.

Unfortunately, drivers can cause problems, particularly when they are used with a new operating system (this invariably introduces technologies that the driver's devices were not designed for). In most cases they will install without problems and the devices will appear to be functioning. However, behind the scenes the drivers may well be the cause of incompatibility issues that can lead to both instability and loss of system performance.

In an effort to prevent this, Windows displays a warning message when it detects that a potentially problematic driver is being installed. However, it is a fact that most users ignore these messages and install the driver regardless. If you've done this yourself, you should be aware that you may well have compromised your system.

So, to be quite sure that the PC is running at its best, you must uninstall all non-certified Windows drivers and replace them with ones that are. To do this:

 Go to the **Search box** on the Taskbar and type "verifier"

 Click the **Verifier** search result, then click **Yes**

 Select **Create standard settings** and click **Next**

Upgrading your device drivers is not just important for the operating system – in many cases, the devices will then perform better too.

If Windows freezes, or is producing frequent Stop Errors, check if the problem is being caused by a faulty driver.

Drivers that are certified for use with Windows have been tested by Windows Hardware Quality Labs (WHQL). They are commonly referred to as "signed drivers" as they have been digitally tagged as such.

Driver Verifier Manager   ✕

Select a task

◉ Create standard settings

4   In the next dialog box, select **Automatically select unsigned drivers** and click **Next**

Driver Verifier Manager   ✕

Select what drivers to verify

◉ Automatically select unsigned drivers

○ Automatically select drivers built for older versions of Windows

Please wait

Searching for unsigned drivers...

○ Automatically select all drive

[Cancel   ]

○ Select driver names from a list

Click Next to verify all unsigned drivers installed on this computer. A list of these drivers will be displayed.

Click Back to review or change the settings you want to create.

[< Back]   [Next >]   [Cancel]

If the search discovers any unsigned drivers they will be listed for you to verify. While they may be fine, these drivers are all potential causes of system problems. Therefore, if you want to be absolutely certain that your computer is stable, and performing as well as possible, you will have to either replace them all with Windows-certified versions, or uninstall them.

To this end, visit the websites of the devices' manufacturers and look for updated drivers certified for use with Windows 10. Download and install them. If a manufacturer doesn't provide a Windows 10 driver, ideally you should replace the device with one from a manufacturer that does.

Many users assume that system crashes and lockups are due to faults in the operating system. The reality is that the majority of them are caused by uncertified hardware drivers or low-quality memory.

Corrupt signed drivers may also cause problems. Choose the option to **Select driver names from a list** to verify individual drivers.

If you can't find a Windows 10 driver, one designed for use with Windows 8.1 will almost certainly be OK.

35

Prioritize CPU Resources

"Priority" is the measure that Windows uses to determine the amount of CPU time that each application receives. By default, most applications are set to the **Normal** priority level, so by changing a specific program to a higher level you can effectively boost its performance. This is useful when you are using several applications simultaneously (multitasking):

Beware

The highest priority setting is **Realtime**. This will give an application the same priority as critical system services. We recommend that you do NOT use this, as doing so can render your system unstable.

 Run the program to be prioritized then open the **Task Manager** (**Ctrl + Shift + Esc**)

 Click **More details**, if tabs are not visible, then choose the **Details** tab

Don't forget

You can also set lower priority levels for your applications.

Right-click on the app you want to prioritize and select **Set priority** to see options ranging from **Low** to **Realtime** priority level

Select the priority level you want for that application then click **Change priority** and close the **Task Manager**

Hot tip

If you have an open program that is accessed infrequently, giving it a lower priority will increase the CPU resources available for more frequently-used applications.

Note that changes to priority level are not permanent; they are effective only while the program is running. If you close it and then open it again, it will have reverted to the default setting.

36

Third-Party Software

Having tweaked Windows to give improved performance, you should now look at your PC's applications. These can also be the cause of performance issues.

Program Overload

The first thing to examine is the number of programs you have installed. The more there are, the slower your PC is going to be, even if they are not being used. If this puzzles you, be aware that many applications (or parts of them) run unseen in the background. So the more software you install, inevitably the more of these background applications there will be. Not only do they slow system performance, they also affect Shutdown and Startup speeds. Examine the number of programs installed as described on page 31. Alternatively, go to **Programs and Features** in the **Control Panel**.

Malware

Malware is a term that encompasses invasive software, such as adware, spyware and browser hijackers. Apart from compromising your PC's security and intruding on your privacy, they can also slow your internet activities considerably and, in the case of hijackers, can have a real impact on the PC's performance.

The **Windows Defender** utility is Windows 10's answer to this problem, which is enabled by default. In theory, this application should keep your system clean of all viruses and malware. In practice, however, it may not do so. Just as email spammers are constantly devising new ways to circumvent spam filters and other safeguards, the authors of viruses/malware are doing the same with anti-virus programs.

You have two ways to approach this problem: prevention or cure. To prevent malware getting onto your PC, avoid:

- Downloading anything from the internet unless you are quite sure about the source

- Browsing the internet with any of your web browser's security features turned off

- Installing software from unverifiable sources

If you must do any of the above, or already have, scan your system with anti-virus and anti-malware programs.

No anti-malware program is perfect, so to ensure your system is as clean as possible, we suggest you use two.

The **Spybot Search & Destroy** anti-malware program is available free at safer-networking.org

The **Malwarebytes** anti-malware program is available free at malwarebytes.org

Refresh the PC

There comes a time in the life of any well-used computer when it will benefit hugely from a good clear out. Over time, files are created and deleted, programs are installed and uninstalled, the inevitable crashes occur, and users do things they shouldn't. A PC can become clogged up with redundant and useless data, long-forgotten files, programs, and broken shortcuts. Furthermore, essential system or program files may have gone missing or been corrupted. At best, this will be the cause of irritating little faults and problems and, at worst, a serious decrease in system performance or loss of functionality.

There is absolutely nothing that can be done about this, no matter how carefully you maintain the PC. Traditionally, the only effective solution to this problem has been a clean install, i.e. backing up all the data on the PC, reformatting the hard drive (which wipes the drive clean), installing a new copy of Windows, and then reinstalling the backed up data and programs.

It is a procedure that returns the PC to an "as new" condition but does require a level of technical expertise that most users simply don't have. However, Windows 10 includes a **Reset this PC** utility that can be used to refresh your PC's operating system, or to completely renew the state of your entire PC. Here, we look at how to refresh your PC to rejuvenate the operating system. We look at the latter on page 205.

Virtually all problems that occur with Windows can be repaired.

The **Reset this PC** utility is new in Windows 10 and has undergone refinement since its introduction, to make it easier to refresh your PC.

It is almost always easier to simply revert the system to a state prior to a fault manifesting itself than it is to isolate and repair the fault.

1 Access the utility by going to **Start** > **Settings** > **Update & Security**. Select the **Recovery** item on the left pane then, under **Reset this PC** on the right pane, click the **Get started** button

Settings	— □ ×
⚙ Home	**Reset this PC**
Find a setting 🔍	If your PC isn't running well, resetting it might help. This lets you choose to keep your files or remove them, and then reinstalls Windows.
Update & security	[Get started]
↻ Windows Update	
▼ Windows Defender	**Advanced startup**
⌃ Backup	Start up from a device or disc (such as a USB drive or DVD), change your PC's firmware settings, change Windows startup settings, or restore Windows from a system image. This will restart your PC.
↺ Recovery	[Restart now]
⊘ Activation	
🖥 Find My Device	**More recovery options**
⫿ For developers	Learn how to start fresh with a clean installation of Windows
ஃ Windows Insider Program	

2 You are then presented with these two options:

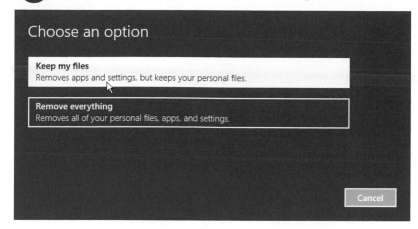

Choose an option

Keep my files
Removes apps and settings, but keeps your personal files.

Remove everything
Removes all of your personal files, apps, and settings.

Cancel

The option to **Keep my files** allows you to refresh your PC. This is what will happen if you run the utility using that option:

- **Your files and personalization settings won't change** – this means that your data will not be deleted, and that any changes you have made to the default personalization settings will be retained. The former is the big plus here, as it means you do not have to make a backup of your data and then reinstall it afterwards.

- **The PC's settings will be changed back to their defaults** – this means that Windows 10 will be deleted and replaced by a new copy. Any configuration changes made to Windows settings will be lost.

- **Apps from the Windows Store will be kept** – apps installed from the Windows Store will not be deleted.

- **Apps you installed from discs or websites will be removed** – all third-party software will be deleted.

Effectively then, the **Reset this PC** utility will install a new copy of Windows 10 while retaining the user's data and personalization settings. Everything else will be deleted. The big drawback is that users will probably have to reinstall/reconfigure most of their software, and reconfigure various Windows settings. That said, it will still be much quicker than doing a clean install as described on pages 125-126.

A big advantage of the **Reset this PC** utility is speed. It can reinstall Windows 10 in a fraction of the time taken by the original installer process.

The system refresh only replaces Windows 10 system files and settings.

39

The big drawback of the **Reset this PC** utility is that users will have to reinstall/reconfigure probably most of their software, and reconfigure various Windows settings.

...cont'd

 3 Select the option to **Keep my files**. If you recently upgraded to Windows 10 you will be warned that you will no longer be able to revert to the previous version of Windows after the reset. Click **Next** to continue

Hot tip

Make a note of the applications that you have installed before the reset so you remember to reinstall them all later.

 4 Now, click **Reset** to proceed

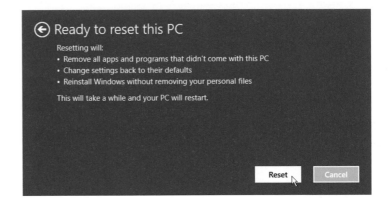

Don't forget

Device drivers for hardware may need to be reinstalled after the reset.

 5 The PC will now reboot and refresh your system

 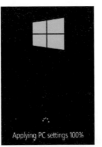 

Hot tip

Once the reset process has begun, you can safely leave it to proceed unattended.

3 Startup & Shutdown

Don't you just hate it when your PC insists on taking its own sweet time to start up and shut down? The procedures in this chapter will teach it some manners and ensure that its laggardly ways are a thing of the past.

Quick Boot

When a computer is booted up, the BIOS (Basic Input/Output System) chip on the motherboard checks and initializes the system's hardware. It then searches all the drives (hard drive, CD/DVD drive, USB drives, etc.) for the operating system.

This tip ensures that it goes immediately to the drive on which the operating system is loaded, i.e. the hard drive, thus saving time:

Hot tip

The key to enter the BIOS setup is shown on the boot screen. With an AWARD BIOS it is usually **Delete**, and with an AMI BIOS it is usually **F2**. If you are unsure, try holding down one or more keys to cause a stuck key error – you may then be offered the option to continue boot or enter BIOS setup.

1 Start the PC and when you see text on the screen, press the key needed to enter the BIOS setup program (see first Hot tip)

2 Using the arrow keys, open the **Advanced BIOS Features** page and press **Enter**

42

Hot tip

You can reach the BIOS setup program from Windows 10 via **Settings** > **Update & security** > **Recovery** and click (under **Advanced startup**) **Restart now**. After the system restarts, choose **Troubleshoot** > **Advanced options** then choose **Startup Settings**, **Restart**, and hit the key to enter BIOS setup or choose **UEFI Firmware Settings**.

```
              Phoenix - AwardBIOS CMOS Setup Utility

 Virus Warning                 [Disabled]
 CPU Internal Cache            [Enabled]      Item Help
 External Cache                [Enabled]
 CPU L2 Cache ECC Checking     [Enabled]
 Processor Number Feature      [Enabled]    Select Your Boot
 Quick Power On Self Test      [Disabled]   Device Priority
 First Boot Device             [HDD-0]
 Second Boot Device            [CDROM]
 Third Boot Device             [Floppy]
 Boot Other Device             [Enabled]
 Swap Floppy Drive             [Disabled]
 Boot Up NumLock Status        [On]
 Gate A20 Option               [Fast]
 Ata 66/100 IDE Cable Msg.     [Enabled]
 Typematic Rate Setting        [Disabled]
 Security Option               [Setup]
 OS Select For DRAM > 64MB     [Non-OS2]

 Esc : Quit
 F10 : Save & Exit Setup

              Virus Protection, Boot Sequence...
```

3 Scroll to **First Boot Device** and use the **Page Up/Page Down** keys to cycle through the options and select **HDD-0**. Note that this only applies if you have just one drive in your PC – if you have more, you will need to choose the one Windows is installed on

The description and steps above (and on page 43) relates to an AWARD BIOS. Users with a BIOS from other manufacturers will find that the terminology used, and page layouts, will differ.

BIOS Speed Boost

Every BIOS has a diagnostic utility called the Power On Self Test (POST), which checks that vital parts of the system, such as the video and memory, are functioning correctly. If there is a problem, it will warn the user accordingly in the form of a series of coded beeps (beep codes) or an error message.

However, the BIOS can be configured to skip through certain non-essential parts of the POST, thus speeding up boot time considerably:

1 In the BIOS setup program, open the **Advanced BIOS Features** page

```
        Phoenix - AwardBIOS CMOS Setup Utility

Virus Warning                [Disabled]
CPU Internal Cache           [Enabled]      Item Help
External Cache               [Enabled]
CPU L2 Cache ECC Checking    [Enabled]
Processor Number Feature     [Enabled]      Select Your Boot
Quick Power On Self Test     [Enabled]      Device Priority
First Boot Device            [HDD-0]
Second Boot Device           [CDROM]
Third Boot Device            [Floppy]
Boot Other Device            [Enabled]
Swap Floppy Drive            [Disabled]
Boot Up NumLock Status       [On]
Gate A20 Option              [Fast]
Ata 66/100 IDE Cable Msg.    [Enabled]
Typematic Rate Setting       [Disabled]
Security Option              [Setup]
OS Select For DRAM > 64MB    [Non-OS2]

Esc : Quit
F10 : Save & Exit Setup

        Virus Protection, Boot Sequence...
```

2 Scroll to **Quick Power On Self Test** and select **Enabled**

3 Save your change then exit the BIOS setup program

Amongst other things, this will make the BIOS skip the memory test that occurs when you turn on your PC. It's a very basic test and the chances are, if you really do have bad memory, the test won't catch it anyway.

Note that some BIOSs have the **Quick Power On Self Test** enabled by default. Not all do though, so check it out.

Beep codes vary but an AWARD BIOS includes:

- **Repeating mid-tone**
  Memory error – check for missing or improperly seated memory.

- **Repeating alternate high-tone/low-tone**
  CPU error– check for damaged, overheating, or improperly seated CPU.

- **Beep 1 long, 2 short**
  Video adapter error – check for an improperly seated video card or disconnected monitor.

43

This setting has various names depending on the BIOS manufacturer. Examples are: **Perform Quick Memory Test**, **Quick Boot**, and **Quick Power On Self Test**.

Disable Unused Hardware

Every time a computer is switched on, its hardware has to be detected and initialized by the BIOS. Thus, the more devices there are, the longer the PC takes to boot up.

While most of the PC's hardware is essential for it to run, in virtually all systems there are some devices that are not used. By disabling these, you can increase the PC's boot speed:

 Go to **Control Panel** > **Device Manager**. Here, you will see a list of all the hardware installed on your system

Beware

Don't disable hardware devices in the **Display adapters** and **System devices** categories – these are critical to the operation of your PC.

Hot tip

The webcam device can be disabled, as shown here – unless it is required for video calling or facial recognition, etc.

```
Device Manager                                          —  □  ×
File  Action  View  Help
LAPTOP
  Audio inputs and outputs
  Batteries
  Computer
  Disk drives
  Display adapters
  Human Interface Devices
  IDE ATA/ATAPI controllers
  Imaging devices
     USB Camera      Update Driver Software...
  Keyboards           Disable
  Memory techno       Uninstall
  Mice and other
  Monitors            Scan for hardware changes
  Network adapte
  Portable Devices    Properties
  Print queues
  Processors
  Software devices
  Sound, video and game controllers
  Storage controllers
  System devices
  Universal Serial Bus controllers
```

Go through the list by expanding categories. Disable any devices you do not use by right-clicking the device and clicking **Disable** on the context menu that appears

Examples of devices that are typically unused include:

- **Network adapters** – most motherboards provide an integrated network adapter.
- **Bluetooth controllers** – if you don't use Bluetooth you don't need to have it enabled.
- **Multimedia devices** – integrated video and sound. Many users have dedicated video and sound cards so don't need these.

Hot tip

You may also find unused hardware that can be disabled in the BIOS.

44

Streamline the Fonts Folder

Windows comes with a large number of fonts, all of which are installed in the **Fonts** folder. As each of these fonts is loaded when the PC starts up, the more there are, the longer startup takes to complete. Therefore, you can increase your boot speed by deleting all but the ones used by the system, and the ones you are likely to use:

 Open the **Windows** folder on the **C:** drive and locate the **Fonts** folder. Right-click it, select **Copy** and save it in a backup location

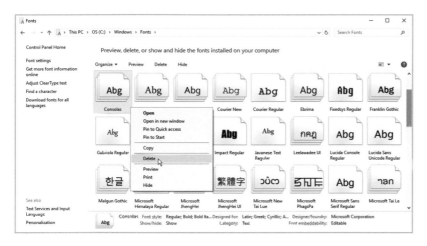

Now, open the original folder and simply work through the fonts, deleting any that are surplus to requirements; this should be the vast majority of them

---

Delete Font ✕

⚠ Microsoft Sans Serif cannot be deleted because it is a protected system font

☐ Don't show this message again   **Close**

Note that some of the fonts are system fonts and are used by the operating system. If you try to delete any of these, you will see the warning "cannot be deleted..." message shown above. Should you subsequently find a need for any of the deleted fonts, just copy them back to the **Fonts** folder from your backup folder.

A font manager can be very useful for users who access the fonts on their systems regularly.

You can download the free NexusFont font manager at **xiles.net**

Be wary of downloading free fonts from the internet. These are often corrupt and may cause your system to lock up completely.

Clear Out the Startup Folder

The next thing to look at is your Startup programs. These are applications that open automatically when Windows starts, and are located in the **Startup** folder. Shortcuts to programs can be placed here by the user to automatically start them with Windows, so they are ready for immediate use. Also, some programs will place a link here automatically when they are installed.

As each of these programs must be loaded before Windows is ready for use, the more items there are in the **Startup** folder, the longer it will take to start Windows.

Check it out as follows:

 Right-click the Taskbar and click **Task Manager** on the context menu to open that utility

 Click the **Startup** tab. You'll see a list of applications that start with Windows, as shown below:

3 Right-click programs you don't need to automatically start with Windows, then click **Disable** from the context menu

However, if there is something you'd rather keep, check the **Startup impact** column to see the impact it has on the PC's Startup speed. If it says **Low** there is really no need to disable it, as its effect will be minimal.

Hot tip

The user's "Startup" folder is located at **C:\ Users*username*\ AppData\Roaming\ Microsoft\Windows\ StartMenu\Programs\ Startup**.

Hot tip

Add a shortcut to a program inside your user's **Startup** folder to have that program automatically open when Windows starts.

Beware

The more programs you have in your **Startup** folder, the longer the PC will take to boot.

Screensavers & Wallpaper

In days gone by, computer monitors were prone to having an impression burnt into the screen by prolonged exposure to a static image. To guard against this unfortunate tendency, screensavers were invented. Apart from serving a useful purpose, they could also be fun. These days, however, that's all they are – fun. They are now completely superfluous in the modern computer system, as monitors are no longer susceptible to damage caused by static images.

Because a screensaver is actually a program, having one enabled means that Windows has one more application to load before it is ready to use. So reduce your PC's startup time by disabling any screensaver that is currently active:

 1 Right-click on the Desktop and choose **Personalize**, then select **Lock screen** > **Screen saver settings** and choose **(None)** from the drop-down box

With regard to wallpaper, these are large image files that have no function other than to make your Desktop look cool. As with screensavers, they slow down the Startup procedure as they also have to be loaded by Windows. Your best option here is to use a solid color as the background:

 2 Right-click on the Desktop and choose **Personalize**, then select **Background** and choose **Solid color** from the drop-down box

Beware

3D screensavers available on the internet can take a long time to load, may contain bugs, and can cause system instability.

Hot tip

Alternatively try **Settings > Ease of Access > Other options > Show Windows background** then set the toggle to **Off** to remove desktop images.

Hot tip

For the least distracting, most productive desktop set the background to a mid-gray solid color.

Shutdown Issues

When a Windows PC takes an unusually long time to shut down, the cause is almost always one of the following:

- A service, or running process, that is slow to close.

- The unloading of user-profile files.

- A non-responding application.

- A corrupted or incompatible device driver.

The first three in the list above have, to a certain degree, been addressed in recent versions of Windows, and therefore do not cause as many problems as they did with earlier versions. That said, on occasion they are still the cause of shutdown issues.

Device drivers are beyond Windows' control, as the decision to install a device driver is made by the user. Windows will warn if a driver being installed is potentially problematic but it cannot stop the installation. This is the biggest cause of Windows shutdown problems (see pages 34-35 for how to eliminate driver issues).

When in this situation, go to the **Control Panel** > **Administrative Tools** > **Component Services**. On the left go to **Event Viewer (Local)** > **Applications and Services Logs** > **Microsoft** > **Windows** > **Diagnostics-Performance** > **Operational**.

Look under the **Task Category** for issues relating to **Shutdown Performance Monitoring**. Clicking an entry will reveal details of the application that is causing a delay in the shutdown process. Click the **Event Log Online Help** link to visit a Microsoft website where you may find more detailed information.

Hot tip

Shutdown issues can be difficult problems to identify. Device drivers are the most likely cause and this is what you should investigate first.

Don't forget

You can open **Device Manager** from the Power User Menu to look for possible device driver problems.

Hot tip

The **Event Log** will also highlight issues that are causing your PC to boot more slowly than it should.

Kill Services Quickly

When a PC's Shut down button is pressed, Windows closes all open applications, including any services that may be running. The length of time Windows allocates for the latter is set by the **WaitToKillServiceTimeout** Registry key – the default setting of which is 5000 ms (5 seconds).

If all running services stop within 5 seconds, the PC shuts down. However, if they don't, the user is presented with a dialog box that offers two options: wait for the service to stop of its own accord, or force it to close. By lowering the default value, you can force tardy services to close more quickly and thus prevent them from slowing down the shutdown procedure.

Alternatively use **Edit** > **Find** in the Registry Editor to locate the **WaitToKillServiceTimeout** Registry key.

1 Press **WinKey + R** and type "regedit" in the Run box, then press **Enter** and agree the UAC dialog

2 When Windows' **Registry Editor** opens, navigate to: **HKEY_LOCAL_MACHINE/SYSTEM/ CurrentControlSet**

Services do need some time to close. The object here is simply to speed up the process a little.

49

3 Expand this item and click the **Control** folder on the left – on the right you will then see the **WaitToKillServiceTimeout** key

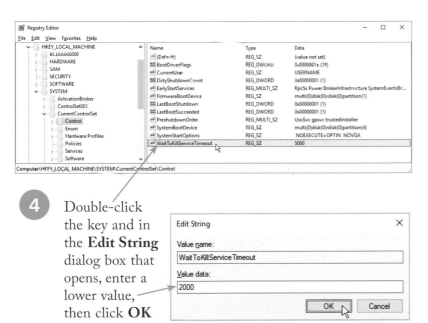

Resist the temptation to set too low a value in the **Edit String**, as this may lead to loss of data.

4 Double-click the key and in the **Edit String** dialog box that opens, enter a lower value, then click **OK**

Put the PC to Sleep

Windows provides an option for closing down your machine, known as "Sleep". This is accessible from **Start** > **Power** > **Sleep**, or by pressing **Ctrl + Alt + Del** and clicking the ⏻ Power button, or by clicking the ⏻ Power button on the **Logon** screen.

On laptops, **Sleep** mode only saves an image to the memory – not to the hard drive as well.

Don't forget

Sleep mode monitors the laptop battery and intelligently transfers the image stored in memory to the hard drive when power runs low.

The **Sleep** mode is basically a combination of the old **Standby** mode and **Hibernate** mode.

In the old **Hibernate** mode, an image of the system was created on the hard drive and then the PC was powered off. The problem was that, in practice, it was not much quicker than just switching off and then back on as normal.

In the old **Standby** mode, an image of the system was created in memory and power was maintained only to essential devices such as the CPU. The problem here was that an application could override Standby and keep the PC running. Also, if power to the PC was lost for some reason, all unsaved data was lost.

Windows **Sleep** mode saves all data in use to both the memory and the hard drive before cutting power to all but a few key components. The procedure takes just a few seconds. When a key is pressed, the mouse moved or the screen tapped, the system is restored from the image stored in the memory. If the machine has been powered off, the system is restored from the image stored on the hard drive on restart. Thus, there is no danger of data loss. Furthermore, and this is the major advantage of **Sleep**, it is quick, taking approximately three seconds to bring the PC back to life.

Sleep mode eliminates the need to switch off a computer between sessions at all. Simply put the machine to sleep at the end of the day, and then have it up-and-running within three seconds the following morning with a single keystroke or mouse click.

Hot tip

Use **Sleep** mode instead of **Shut down** to have your PC ready for work almost instantly at your next session.

4 Productivity

Computers can be used for both entertainment and work. In this chapter we focus on the latter, looking at ways to increase the efficiency with which you use your computer. These will help you to save time, and also be more productive.

Find it Fast

An important part of working efficiently and productively is being able to locate things quickly when needed. The worker who can lay their hand on the right tool when needed will get the job done faster than the one who has to go looking for it.

Working on a PC is much the same, so to make life easier for users in this respect, Windows 10 provides a **Search** utility. This is tightly integrated in the operating system and thus instantly accessible from virtually any location. You will find it in any File Explorer folder and through the Taskbar Search box. One of its best features is that it is contextual, i.e. its search is based on the user's current activity, whether it's searching for utilities in the **Control Panel**, or for files and applications on the hard drive.

Folder Searches

If you already know in which folder the file is located, use the Search box at the top-right of the folder. By default, the search will be restricted to the contents of the **Current folder**. You will also see an option for searching **All subfolders** of the current folder. Next to this is an option for searching the entire computer – use **This PC** when you have no idea where to look.

Don't forget

By default, a folder search will only find content that is located in the folder in which the search is conducted.

Hot tip

Open **File Explorer** then click in its Search box to reveal the **Search Tools** tab options, shown here.

Hot tip

If the Taskbar Search box is not visible, right-click the Taskbar and choose **Cortana** > **Show search box** to reveal it.

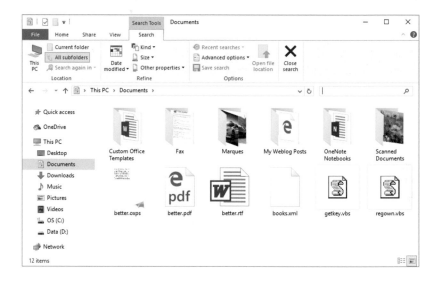

Also available are filters, which help to speed up the search – these appear on the Ribbon when you click in the Search box and enable you to search by various criteria, such as **Date modified**, **Kind**, **Size**, etc. See page 56 for more on filters.

...cont'd

Windows 10 Search

The **Search** function is also available from the Windows 10 Taskbar **Search** box. Just begin typing your query and it will open.

The **Search** results produce a **Best match** suggestion and further **Settings**, **Apps**, **Store**, and **Web** category suggestions. Select an item to view that result, or select any category heading to refine your results. Click the **More** button at the top right of the results panel to filter your results further.

The **Cortana** Personal Digital Assistant also lets you search using voice commands. The **Search** box and **Cortana** both conduct their searches using the Microsoft Bing search engine. However, **Cortana** voice search results are typically displayed in the Microsoft Edge web browser. For example, "find Ferrari" displays a web page listing search results. Voice searches within Windows 10 need to be phrased well to produce the best results. For filenames beginning with the term "Ferrari" try searching with the phrase "find my Ferrari documents", or "find my Ferrari pictures":

You can find and open apps using the Taskbar **Search** box – enter "notepad" then click the **Best match** result to open the **Notepad** app.

You can also open apps using the **Cortana** Personal Digital Assistant – say "Hey Cortana. Open Notepad", if you have set this up in Settings.

53

If **Cortana** is not working or enabled in your country, set your region to "United States" in **Settings** > **Time & language** > **Region & language**.

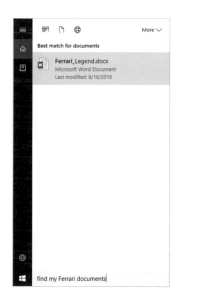

Using Search Aids

Windows 10 provides two very useful tools that enable the user to increase the efficiency with which the Search utility is used.

File Indexer

The first is the Indexing utility. When the operating system is run for the first time, it creates an index of all the files in the most commonly-used locations (note, not the entire computer). As a result, subsequent searches are much faster, as Windows searches the index rather than the computer.

Don't forget

Indexing proceeds in the background and may slow down during periods of user activity.

Hot tip

Adding information to search filters about a file you're looking for will enable the file to be located more quickly.

Beware

If you decide to index the entire computer, be aware that the procedure can take several hours. During this time, system performance may be adversely affected. This only needs to be done once though, so it's not a major deal.

However, users who are in the habit of scattering files all over the place, or adding storage devices to the PC, e.g. a second hard drive, can configure the utility to index any location they wish, or even the entire system.

To do this, go to **Control Panel > Indexing Options**. Click **Modify** to open the **Indexed Locations** dialog, then select the locations to be included in the index.

To further refine indexing, go to **Control Panel > Indexing Options**, then click **Advanced** to open the **Advanced Options** dialog. Select the **Index Settings** tab or **File Types** tab, then choose your indexing preferences.

54

...cont'd

File Tagger

Tags provide a method of invisibly marking selected files. This makes the procedure of subsequently finding and organizing them much quicker and more efficient. Tagging is particularly useful on computers that have lots of images stored on them.

Use this feature as follows:

 Open the folder containing the file to be tagged, click the **View** tab and then click **Details pane** on the menu bar

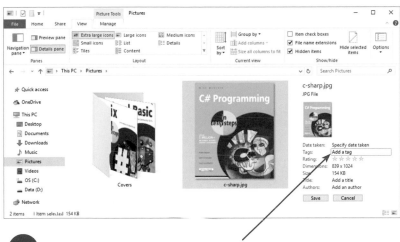

Select the file, click **Add a tag** and enter an appropriate word or phrase. Then, click **Save**

Another way to tag a file is to right-click it, select **Properties** and open the **Details** tab. Then select **Tags** and press any key – this will open a text entry box alongside, as shown below:

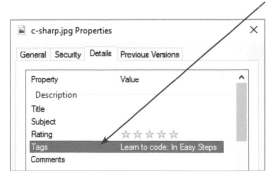

Type your tag into the box. You can also add or change other properties in the same way, e.g. **Title**, **Comments**, etc. These all give you extra options when searching.

Hot tip

You can add multiple tags to a picture. To separate tags, type a semicolon (;) between each tag.

Hot tip

Add a star rating to rank your favorite media files – from one to five stars.

Don't forget

The **Tag** feature does not work with all file types. Microsoft file types, e.g. **.doc** or **.docx** (Word), and some image files work but files from third-party applications don't.

55

Depending on where you're searching, only certain search filters are available. For example, if you're searching the **Documents** library, you'll see different search filters than you would in the **Pictures** library.

You can use several filters in a search and also combine them with regular search terms to refine the search.

Advanced Searching

Searching in Windows 10 can be as simple as typing a few letters in the Search box. However, there are also advanced techniques that can be used, which can be helpful depending on where you're searching and what you're searching for.

Operators

One method of refining a search is to use the operators **AND**, **OR**, and **NOT**. These must be typed in capital letters. The table below shows how they work:

Operator	Example	Action
AND	gold AND mine	Finds files that contain both of the words "gold" and "mine"
NOT	gold NOT mine	Finds files that contain the word "gold" but not "mine"
OR	gold OR mine	Finds files that contain either of the words "gold" or "mine"

Search Filters

Search filters are a feature that find the location of files by defining specific properties, e.g. author, file size, date, etc. To use a filter, open the folder to be searched and then click in the Search box. This opens the **Search Tools** tab on the toolbar. Choose the required filter and select from the available options. For example, choose the **Date modified** filter and the **Today** option, as shown here:

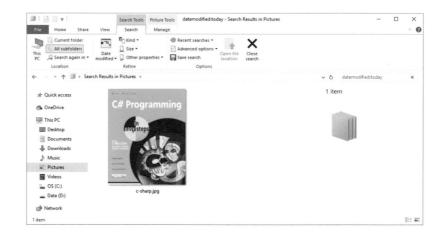

Keywords

If you cannot see the filter you need when you click in the Search box, try a keyword instead. Typically, this requires a property name to be specified, then a colon, sometimes an operator, and then a value. Some examples are shown below:

Example Search Term	Action
System.FileName:~<"report"	Finds files with names beginning with "report". The ~< means "begins with"
System.FileName:="monthly report.doc"	Finds files named "monthly report.doc". The = means "matches exactly"
System.FileName:~="pro"	Finds files with names containing the word "pro" or the characters "pro" as part of another word (such as "process" or "procedure"). The ~= means "contains"
System.Kind:<>video	Finds files that aren't videos. The <> means "is not"
System.DateModified: 09/24/2015	Finds files that were modified on that date. You can also type "System.DateModified:2015" to find files changed at any time during that year
System.Author:~!"john"	Finds files whose authors don't have "john" in their name. The ~! means "doesn't contain"
System.Size:<1gb	Finds files less than 1GB in size
System.Size:>5gb	Finds files more than 5GB in size

You can also use the operators **AND**, **OR**, and **NOT** to combine search keywords.

Example Search Term	Action
System.Author:john AND dave	Finds files authored by John as well as files that include Dave
System.Author:john AND System.DateModified:>2015	Finds only files that are authored by John after 2015
System.Author:"john parker"	Finds files that are authored by John Parker
System.Author:(john* AND dave)	Files that have either John and Dave or Dave and John listed as authors

Hot tip

You can use a **?** wildcard for a single character ("rep?rt") and an asterisk * for multiple characters ("rep*").

Don't forget

System.FileName searches are case-sensitive, so "Report.doc" and "report.doc" are seen as different files.

Hot tip

In the final example on the left, note how adding parentheses can change the effect of a search term.

More Right-Click Options

The right-click context menu offers many useful options. Let's see how to add some more options:

Move To Folder and Copy To Folder

The right-click **Cut** and **Copy** commands allow you to copy and move files to different locations. However, you have to go to the desired location to complete the operation. Here's a faster way:

A new **Copy To folder...** context menu option will let you easily create a duplicate file in your chosen location.

A new **Move To folder...** context menu option will let you easily relocate a selected file to your chosen location.

These string values are identical, except for **630** and **631** in the strings.

 Open the Registry Editor by going to the Taskbar Search box and typing "regedit". Then, locate the following key: **HKEY_CLASSES_ROOT\AllFilesystemObjects\ shellex\ContextMenuHandlers**

 Right-click the **ContextMenuHandlers** folder and select **New > Key**. Name the key "Copy To"

3 Double-click the new key's **Default** icon in the right pane, to open its **Edit String** dialog, then precisely enter the following **Value data** string value: **{C2FBB630-2971-11D1-A18C-00C04FD75D13}**

4 Repeat the above procedure, this time naming the key "Move To" and precisely enter the following string value: **{C2FBB631-2971-11D1-A18C-00C04FD75D13}**

 Close the Registry Editor. Now, right-click a folder or file and you will see new **Copy To folder...** and **Move To folder...** options

58

...cont'd

Add options to the Send to menu

The **Send to** menu provides another very useful method of quickly relocating data. It can also be used to open a file with which an application is not associated. For example, if your image files open with the Windows 10 **Photos** app by default, you can use the **Send to** feature to open them with a different program.

If an application you would like to use in this way is not in the default **Send to** list, you can add it as described below:

1. The **Send to** folder is hidden by default. To reveal it, open **Control Panel** > **File Explorer Options** > **View**, then select **Show hidden files, folders, and drives**

2. Go to your **C:** drive, open the **Users** folder and click your username. Then click **AppData** > **Roaming** > **Microsoft** > **Windows** to now see the **Send to** folder

3. In the **Send to** folder, create shortcuts to the applications you want to add to the **Send to** menu. For example, to **C:\Windows\System32\mspaint.exe** for the **Paint** app

4. When you have finished, close the folder and return to the Desktop. Your applications will now be available from the **Send to** menu

Quickly jump to the **Send to** folder by typing **%appdata%\microsoft\windows\sendto** into the Run box or File Explorer address bar.

Right-click on an app icon and choose **Open File Location** to help discover its path address on your system.

59

While the majority of programs work with the **Send to** feature, not all do. So if you try this and the program doesn't appear in the **Send to** list, don't waste time trying to figure out why. For example, programs from Microsoft Office Suites, such as Word, Excel and PowerPoint.

Quick File Selection

The traditional way of selecting a bunch of files is to drag a box around them with the left mouse button depressed. Individual files are selected by holding down the **Ctrl** key.

Windows 10 provides a better way:

 1 Go to **Control Panel** and open the **File Explorer Options** utility. Then, click the **View** tab

2 Scroll down the list and check the **Use check boxes to select items** option

3 Now, click the **Apply** button to implement your change

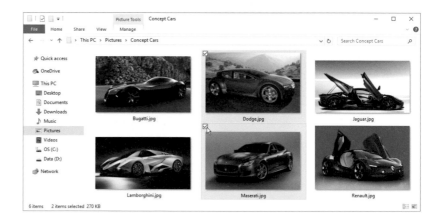

The next time you open a folder, hovering the mouse over each file opens a check box to the left of the file. Simply check the box to select the file. This method is quicker and more precise.

To deselect all check box-selected files in a folder, left-click once in an empty part of the folder.

Check boxes will appear beside each file in any **File Explorer** view – for any size Icons, List, Details, Tiles, or Contents.

You can still select files in the traditional way by dragging a box around the file icons.

Batch Renaming of Files

Have you ever been in a situation in which you have a bunch of related files with an assortment of meaningless or unrelated names? To make order of them, you have to individually rename each file, which can be a tedious task.

Well, all that is now a thing of the past. Windows 10 provides you with a means of sequentially renaming any number of files with the minimum of effort:

1   Select the files to be renamed

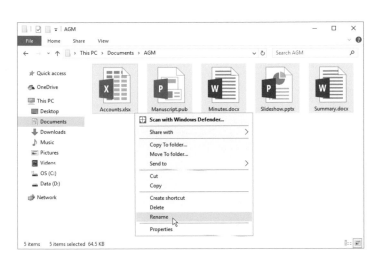

Click anywhere in the folder then press the **Ctrl + A** keyboard shortcut to quickly select all files.

2   Right-click the first file in the list and click **Rename**. Type in a suitable name, for example "Meeting", then click anywhere in the folder. The files will now all be automatically renamed, as shown below:

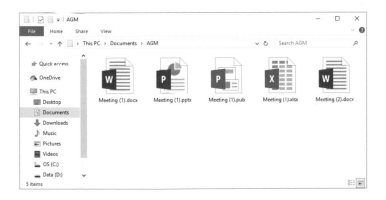

You can optionally use the Windows check box feature to select files.

Notice that these automatically renamed files are named alike but are also sequentially numbered for like file types, such as **.docx**.

Change/Set File Associations

All files are designed to be opened with a specific type of program. For example, graphics files such as JPEG and GIF can only be opened by a graphics-editing program, e.g. **Paint**, or with an image viewer, such as Windows 10's **Photos** app.

A common problem that many users experience is when they install a program on their PC that automatically makes itself the default program for opening related files. If the user prefers the original program, he or she will have to reassociate the file type in question. Alternatively, the user might want to set a different program as the default:

You can open a file with a program not associated as its default by right-clicking the file and choosing from the **Open with** options.

If a newly-installed program has rudely hi-jacked your favorite files, you can re-associate those files with your favorite program.

 Go to **Control Panel** > **Default Programs**. Click **Associate a file type or protocol with a specific program**

 Select the file type from the list, then click the **Change program** button

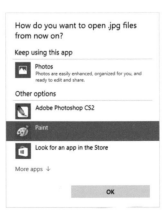

3 You will now see a list of programs on the PC capable of opening the file. Select the one you want to associate with the file type

Another way to associate programs is to right-click a file then choose **Properties** > **General** tab and click the **Change** button – select the one you want.

Close Non-Responding Programs

Every computer user has experienced this. You close a program but instead of disappearing gracefully and without fuss, it insists on hanging around. You click the red **X** button repeatedly but it refuses to go.

When this happens, after a few moments a dialog box will open asking if you want to wait until the program closes or whether you want to close it yourself. The latter option will usually do the trick; however, it doesn't always work.

In this situation, do the following:

 Right-click the Taskbar and click **Task Manager**

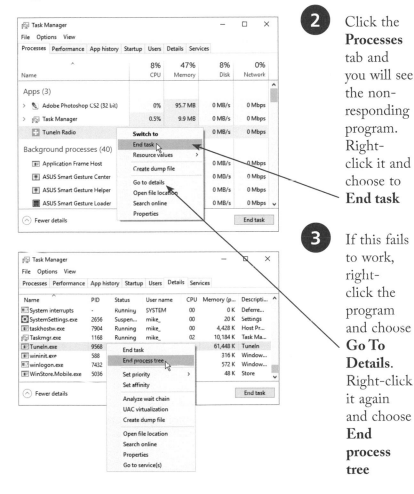

Beware

If you haven't already saved your data, closing a non-responding application with the **Task Manager** may result in you losing that data.

2 Click the **Processes** tab and you will see the non-responding program. Right-click it and choose to **End task**

Hot tip

If the Desktop is unresponsive just press **Ctrl + Alt + Delete** then select **Task Manager** to open the Task Manager dialog.

3 If this fails to work, right-click the program and choose **Go To Details**. Right-click it again and choose **End process tree**

Hot tip

Every now and again, you will open a web page that causes your browser to stop responding. Use this tip to close it.

Create Your Own Toolbars

Most people create shortcuts on the Desktop for frequently used programs, thus enabling them to be accessed quickly. The problem with this is that you can end up with a Desktop cluttered with many icons. Here's another way:

Hot tip

Your custom toolbar can contain links to both frequently used apps and frequently used folders.

Don't forget

Toolbars provide a useful means of quickly accessing your programs, and also keeping the Desktop free of clutter.

Hot tip

Open your custom toolbar and click any item to launch a favorite app or favorite folder.

1. Create a new folder and place shortcuts to the required applications in the folder. Give it a suitable name and then close it

2. Right-click the Taskbar and select **Toolbars > New toolbar...** to create a custom toolbar

3. Browse to the new folder location, then select the folder and click the **Select Folder** button

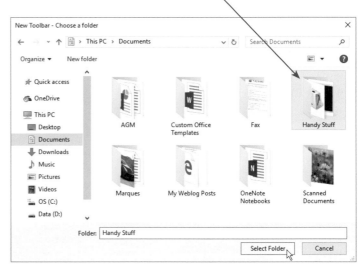

4. A toolbar containing your shortcuts appears to the left of the notification area. Click the chevrons to access them

Create a Customized Control Panel

The **Control Panel** is a very useful and often overlooked section of Windows operating systems. From here, you can access settings that affect virtually all aspects of the computer.

It does, however, contain quite a few applications that will be of no interest to the average user – **Sync Center**, **Credential Manager**, and **Speech Recognition** are typical examples. There are others though, such as **Internet Options**, **System**, and **Administrative Tools**, that many people will use frequently.

This tip will give you quick access to the ones you use and allow you to forget about the ones you don't:

1 Create a new folder on the Desktop and name it "Custom Control Panel"

2 Open **Control Panel** (the real one) and create desktop shortcuts to the applications you use (right-click and select **Create Shortcut**)

3 Close **Control Panel** and go back to the Desktop. Now, drag the shortcuts to the **Custom Control Panel** folder

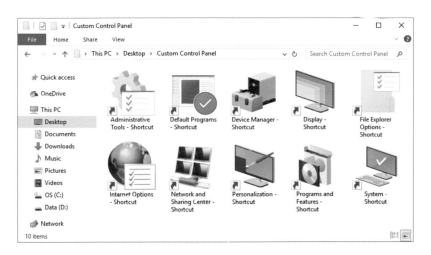

You now have a **Custom Control Panel** on the Desktop that contains only the applications that you use. This lets you locate the items quickly instead of having to search through a long list.

Look through the **Control Panel** utilities and you may find a lot of Windows features and settings that you didn't even know existed.

You cannot save shortcuts in the actual **Control Panel** – accept the dialog suggestion to save them on the Desktop instead.

You can also use your new **Custom Control Panel** folder to create a space-saving custom toolbar on the Taskbar.

Organize Your Data

Windows 10 includes a feature known as **Libraries**. This is a data management system that enables the user to quickly and easily organize specific types of data, e.g. images, documents, videos, etc.

The concept behind this is that of a single folder known as a "library", which contains user-defined subfolders. The subfolders are not actually stored in the library, though – they are still in their original locations. These could be a different hard drive, a flash drive or even a separate PC (in the case of a networked system). However, they are all instantly accessible from the library folder. Furthermore, any changes to the contents of the subfolders, wherever they may be, are dynamically updated in the library.

Windows typically starts you off with four default libraries – **Documents**, **Music**, **Pictures**, and **Videos**, which cover the main file types. These can be accessed on the Navigation pane of any **File Explorer** window by selecting **View** > **Navigation pane** > **Show libraries**. Should you wish to create a new library, you can do so by clicking on **Libraries** in the Navigation pane, then right-clicking in the content pane and selecting **New** > **Library**.

To add content to a new library, open it and click **Include a folder**. To add content to an existing library, click **Library tools** at the top of the window and then **Manage** > **Manage library**.

Hot tip

If you like things neat and tidy, or need to organize your data efficiently, Windows' **Libraries** feature is just what you need.

Hot tip

Windows indexes all library folders to enable fast searching.

Hot tip

Used in conjunction, Windows' **Tags** feature (see page 55) and **Libraries** provide a quick method of assimilating data and then efficiently organizing it into easily-accessible locations.

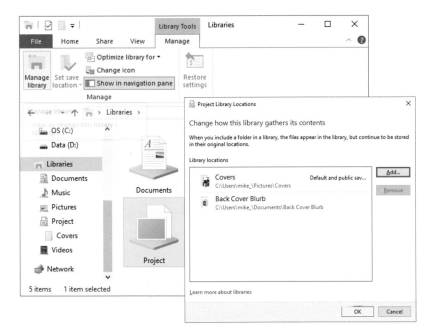

Use Apps from Any Source

Windows 10 will only allow the user to install apps from trusted sources, i.e. they have to be digitally signed. This means they must be downloaded from the Windows Store – try installing an app from any other source and you won't be able to. The reasoning behind this is that it helps protect the user's security.

This is all well and good, and will indeed protect many users from themselves. However, for advanced users who are well aware of the risks and know how to deal with them, this is an unwelcome restriction that limits their use of the PC.

There is a way of circumventing this restriction, though. Do it as described below:

1 Press **WinKey + R** to open the Run box, then type in "gpedit.msc" and hit **Enter**

2 When the **Local Group Policy Editor** opens, choose **Computer Configuration** > **Administrative Templates** > **Windows Components** > **App Package Deployment**

3 On the right pane, double-click **Allow all trusted apps to install** then select **Enabled** and click **Apply** > **OK**

You will now be able to install apps from any source. Just remember that you need to be careful if you don't want to end up with a virus/malware-infested computer.

The **Local Group Policy Editor** utility is only available in Windows 10 Pro and Windows 10 Enterprise editions.

You can also enter "gpedit.msc" into the Taskbar Search box to open the **Local Group Policy Editor** utility.

The **Local Group Policy Editor** utility is a **Microsoft Management Console (MMC)** snap-in, which can be used to customize the interface, restrict access to certain areas, specify security settings, and lots more.

Navigation Pane Folders

A very useful feature found in Windows **File Explorer** is the **Navigation pane** on the left-hand side of the window.

By default, the **Navigation pane** displays the commonly-accessed locations shown here on the right.

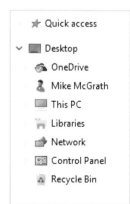

> ⭐ Quick access

> ☁ OneDrive

> 🖥 This PC

> 📁 Network

For those of you who wish to make the most of the **Navigation pane**, you may wish to see a more comprehensive selection of folders there:

If the **Navigation pane** is not visible in File Explorer, click **View** > **Navigation pane** on the menu bar to see it.

 Open **File Explorer** in any folder and click the **View** tab on the menu bar

 At the far-right, you'll see **Options**. Click the arrow below **Options** to open the **Folder Options** dialog box

Press **Ctrl + Shift + E** to expand the **Navigation pane** contents at your current folder location.

 Select the **Folder Options** > **View** tab then scroll down to the **Navigation pane** section and check **Show all folders**

 Click the **Apply** button to implement your changes, then OK to close the **Folder Options** dialog

Click any folder in the **Navigation pane** and see the number of items contained in that folder displayed on the **File Explorer** status bar.

5 Now, see that the **Navigation pane** contains a more comprehensive selection of folders – listed under the **Desktop** folder

⭐ Quick access

∨ 🖥 Desktop

    ☁ OneDrive

    👤 Mike McGrath

    🖥 This PC

    📚 Libraries

    📁 Network

    🖳 Control Panel

    🗑 Recycle Bin

Snap Your Apps

Universal Windows apps are designed to look great full-screen. However, with the large wide-screen monitors available today, many users will find it irritating to have their entire desktop real-estate taken up by just one program.

To address this issue, Windows 10 offers a feature called **Snap**, which enables users to run up to four apps side-by-side. The actual number depends on the monitor's resolution. Resolutions of 2,560 x 1,440 pixels can snap four apps. Resolutions less than this will only be able to snap two or three.

Snap an app in Windows 10, and the new **Snap Assist** feature will display thumbnails of your other open app windows. Click on a thumbnail of your choice to see that app window "**Snap**" to a vacant part of the display screen.

Here, two apps are snapped – the Weather app and the Maps app

To set this up:

1 Open the first app then click its window Title bar and drag it out to the left edge of the screen. Release the mouse button to see the app window snap to the left half of the screen

2 Now, open the second app and drag it out to the right edge of the screen. Release the mouse button to see the app window snap to the right half of the screen

If the screen's resolution allows, you can repeat this with a third or fourth app, displaying one app in each corner. It's as easy as that.

One way in which this feature may prove to be useful is that it enables a Universal Windows app to be run alongside a traditional Windows app. For example, you can browse the web with **Microsoft Edge** and make notes alongside in **Notepad**.

If your resolution allows four-corner Snap, just drag a window to any corner of the screen and it will "**Snap**" to one quarter of the display.

For the Windows **Snap** feature to work, the device must have a screen width of at least 1366 pixels. If you are having problems, check this out by going to **Control Panel** > **Display** > **Adjust Resolution**.

Miscellaneous Tips

Switch to Full-Screen mode
When you're working in a folder that contains a large number of files, you can reduce the amount of scrolling necessary by simply pressing the **F11** function key. This switches the folder to full-screen view. Press **F11** again to revert to the normal view.

Access an inaccessible PC
When you're working in full-screen mode, both the Desktop and Taskbar are hidden. Also, many games do the same by running permanently in full-screen mode.

If you need to open a file or program when in this situation, you can access the PC by pressing the Windows key (**WinKey**).

Whether in Desktop or Tablet mode, this opens the **Start** menu. Press the **WinKey** again to close the **Start** menu.

Restore previous folders at logon
If you log off with a bunch of folders open, Windows closes them all for you. If you want the folders to reopen in their original size and position when you log on again, do this:

 Go to **Control Panel** > **File Explorer Options**, then click the **View** tab to see a list of **Advanced settings**

 Check the **Restore previous folder windows at logon** box

 Click the **Apply** button to implement your choice, then click OK

 Log off then log back on to see your open folders retained

If you want to rename a file, rather than right-clicking it and choosing **Rename**, select it with the mouse then press the **F2** function key.

You can use the **Up** and **Down** arrow keys to move through the **Start** menu, then hit **Enter** to launch an app.

Have you ever needed to insert the date and time in a **Notepad** document? Here's an easy way – rather than typing it, just press the **F5** function key.

70

File Explorer Options ✕

General   View   Search

Folder views
You can apply this view (such as Details or Icons) to all folders of this type.

Apply to Folders   Reset Folders

Advanced settings:
☐ Hide extensions for known file types
☑ Hide folder merge conflicts
☑ Hide protected operating system files (Recommended)
☐ Launch folder windows in a separate process
☑ Restore previous folder windows at logon
☑ Show drive letters
☐ Show encrypted or compressed NTFS files in color
☑ Show pop-up description for folder and desktop items
☑ Show preview handlers in preview pane
☑ Show status bar
☑ Show sync provider notifications
☐ Use check boxes to select items

Restore Defaults

OK   Cancel   Apply

Bypass the Recycle Bin
If you can live without the safety net of the **Recycle Bin**, you can speed up file deletion by doing away with it completely:

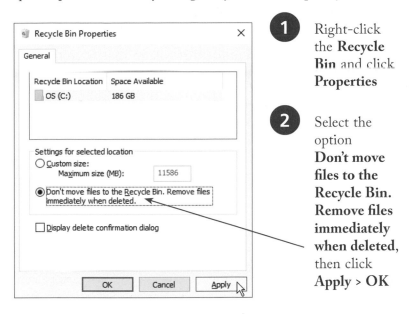

1 Right-click the **Recycle Bin** and click **Properties**

2 Select the option **Don't move files to the Recycle Bin. Remove files immediately when deleted,** then click **Apply > OK**

Another way to bypass the **Recycle Bin** is to hold down the **Shift** key as you click **Delete**.

Select the option for **Display delete confirmation dialog** to guard against accidental deletion of a file.

Start your favorite programs automatically
This tip will enable you to start any application automatically with Windows, so it is up-and-running when the Desktop appears:

1 Press **WinKey + R**. In the Run box, type: **C:\Users*username*\AppData\Roaming\Microsoft\ Windows\Start Menu\Programs\Startup** (where *username* is the name of your profile folder)

2 The **Startup** folder will open – create shortcuts to the programs you want to auto-start. The next time you start the PC, the programs will launch automatically

Quick Zoom
If you want to zoom in on the contents of a folder, instead of using the **View** menu, hold down the **Ctrl** key and scroll the mouse wheel. Move forwards to zoom in and backwards to zoom out. This works in any Windows folder, on the Desktop, in Microsoft Edge, and most third-party applications.

When working in Windows, a quick way to undo your last action (providing you have not bypassed the Recycle Bin) is to press the **Ctrl + Z** keys. For example: if you have deleted a file by mistake. Rather than opening the **Recycle Bin** and searching through it, pressing **Ctrl + Z** will restore the file instantly.

71

...cont'd

Quick Search

You've got a text document open and need to find a specific word, or all instances of one. The Windows **Search** utility isn't much use in this situation.

Rather than read laboriously through the document, just press **Ctrl + F**. This opens a **Find** utility that will go straight to the required word and highlight it for you.

The Microsoft Edge web browser has a similar feature called **Copy Link** on its right-click menu that lets you copy and paste a link as text.

Click the **Find Next** button to find another instance of the word.

The **Copy Link** feature is handy for inserting a link in an email so the recipient can easily jump to a referenced website.

This works in any Windows text document, such as **Notepad**, **WordPad**, and **Journal**. It also works in most word-processors and desktop publishing apps, all **Office** apps and on most web pages.

Copy as path

Here's a handy little feature that can be a real time saver. Now and again, you need to find out the exact path of a file or folder. This could be to change a setting in the Registry, or to copy a link from a network file to share into an email, or other destination.

You can also use the keyboard shortcuts **Ctrl + C** to copy, **Ctrl + X** to cut, and **Ctrl + V** to paste.

The usual way to do this is to right-click the file and choose **Properties**. Next to **Location** in the **General** tab is the file's path you can copy and paste.

A quicker way is to right-click the file or folder while holding the **Shift** key down, and click **Copy as path**. Then go to your destination, right-click and choose **Paste**. Voilà! Job done.

5 Things You Can Do Without

This chapter shows you how

to get rid of, or moderate,

some of the unnecessary

features in Windows 10.

User Account Control (UAC)

User Account Control (**UAC**) is a security feature designed to protect users from themselves, i.e. unwittingly making changes to the system that can compromise its security.

The most obvious manifestations of **UAC** are the "Do you want to allow..." dialog boxes that pop up when the user tries to do certain actions – installing a program, for example – and the **Secure Desktop** (when access to the Desktop is removed).

These dialogs quickly become extremely tiresome, so getting rid of **UAC** (or reducing its level) is perhaps the first thing many users will want to do.

This is actually very simple, as we see below:

1 Go to **Control Panel** > **User Accounts**, then click **Change User Account Control settings**

2 Drag the slider to adjust the level of **UAC** (the bottom of the slider is off completely)

The UAC dialogs were given a colorful new look in the Windows 10 Anniversary Update.

You should not disable **UAC** completely unless you are aware of the security issues involved. It is there for a reason.

74

User Account Control Settings

Choose when to be notified about changes to your computer

User Account Control helps prevent potentially harmful programs from making changes to your computer.
Tell me more about User Account Control settings

Always notify

Never notify me when:
- Apps try to install software or make changes to my computer
- I make changes to Windows settings

Not recommended.

Never notify

OK   Cancel

Notifications

Many people find the notifications that regularly spring up from the System Tray notification area very irritating. Although they do sometimes give useful information, most of the time it is something obvious or that is already known to the user.

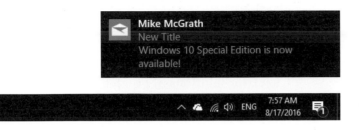

Notifications sometimes offer useful advice. For example, if your hard drive is running low on space, a notification will warn you.

For those of you who can do without these notifications, the solution is as follows:

1 Go to **Settings** > **System** > **Notifications & actions**

2 Drag the toggle buttons to the **Off** position for those types of notification you do not want to receive

Disable notifications at your own risk. We recommend you leave them enabled.

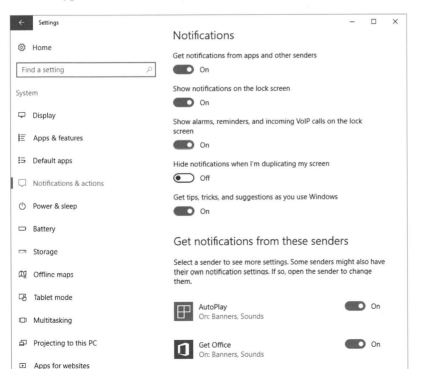

Leave **Get notifications from apps and other senders** turned **On** so you can turn **Off** unwanted individual senders' notifications.

75

Problem Reports

Every time an application experiences an error and is closed down by the system, the **Windows Problem Reporting** utility will spring to life asking if you want to seek a solution from Microsoft. If you're the one in a million who will actually do this, then read no further. If you've no intention of complying though, you'll want to get rid of this irritation as soon as possible:

Take care when editing the Windows Registry as it may compromise your system settings.

Previous versions of Windows provided an option to turn Off Problem Reporting, but Windows 10 prefers you to leave it turned On.

Before you disable Problem Reports, you should be aware that, if it is available, Microsoft will send you the solution to the problem. So while it is undoubtedly irritating, it can help to prevent a repeat occurrence of the problem in the future.

1 Go to **Control Panel** > **Security and Maintenance**, then click on **Maintenance** to expand those settings – see that **Check for solutions to problem reports** is turned **On**

2 Open the Windows Registry Editor (regedit) at **HKEY_LOCAL_MACHINE\SOFTWARE\ Microsoft\Windows\Windows Error Reporting**

3 Right-click in the right pane and choose **New** > **DWORD (32-bit) Value** and name the key "disabled"

4 Double-click this new key, then set its **Value data** to **1** and click **OK**

5 Now, re-open **Control Panel** > **Security and Maintenance**, **Maintenance** and see that the **Check for solutions to problem reports** setting is turned **Off**

Peek

A feature introduced in Windows 7 and continued with Windows 10 is **Peek**. This is a **Show desktop** button located at the bottom right-hand corner of the screen, at the very end of the Taskbar.

When the button is clicked, any open windows are hidden, and the windows reappear when the button is clicked again. Any open windows are also hidden if you simply hover the mouse over the **Show desktop** button – and the windows reappear when the mouse is moved away. While this can be useful, it can also be annoying when the feature is accidentally activated by unintentionally moving the mouse over the **Show desktop** button, and thus hiding the window you are working in.

You can disable the feature by doing the following:

1 Go to **Settings** > **Personalization** then select the Taskbar option from the left pane

2 Drag the toggle button to the **Off** position for the item **Use Peek to preview the desktop when you move your mouse to the Show desktop button at the end of the taskbar**

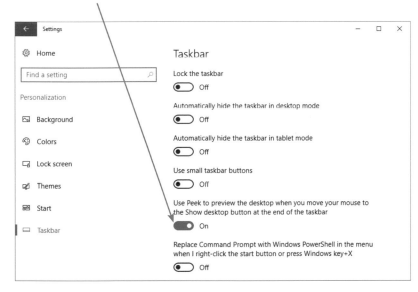

Don't forget

In Windows 7, this feature was known as "Aero Peek". In Windows 10, it is now just **Peek**. The **Show desktop** button does not appear in **Tablet mode** – as it only relates to the Windows **Desktop**.

Hot tip

Use the **Show desktop** button to quickly access icons and shortcuts placed on your **Desktop**.

Hot tip

Alternatively, right-click on the **Show desktop** button and uncheck the **Peek at desktop** option to disable this feature.

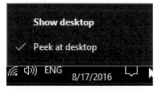

The **Snap** feature simplifies the process of dragging and dropping between two windows, or comparing their content. With **Snap**, you can grab a window and move your mouse to the edge of the screen and the window will resize to fill half the screen. Repeat with the other window to have two side-by-side windows.

Without **Snap**, a considerable amount of mouse movement is needed to resize and position two windows side-by-side.

Snap

Windows 10 features a novel way to arrange your windows. This is known as **Snap** and basically it provides a quick way of resizing and tiling windows (see page 69).

However, like **Peek**, this is a feature that some users may want to disable, as at times it will cause you to resize a window when all you were intending to do was move it to a different part of the screen.

The **Snap** feature can be disabled as follows:

1 Go to **Control Panel** > **Ease of Access Center**

2 Click the **Make the mouse easier to use** link

3 Check the **Prevent windows from being automatically arranged when moved to the edge of the screen** option

4 Click **Apply** > **OK**, then try to **Snap** a window to see this feature is no longer enabled

Lock Screen

Because Windows 10 can be used with touchscreens, and so requires a protective barrier against accidental inputs, Microsoft has built in a user **Lock screen**. However, for users who don't have a touchscreen monitor, this is a superfluous feature.

When you press **WinKey + L** to activate the user **Lock screen**, Windows 10 runs a **LockApp.exe** file on your system. This can be disabled by hiding its location, as described below:

You can customize the **Lock screen** to show app statuses at **Settings > Personalization > Lock screen**.

1 Launch **File Explorer** then navigate to the folder at **C:\Windows\SystemsApps**

2 Next, locate the sub-folder, snappily named **Microsoft.LockApp_cw5n1h2txyewy**

3 Now, rename the sub-folder, such as **Microsoft.LockApp_cw5n1h2txyewy.DISABLED**

Name	Date modified	Type
ContactSupport_cw5n1h2txyewy	8/13/2016 9:36 PM	File folder
Microsoft.AAD.BrokerPlugin_cw5n1h2txyewy	8/13/2016 9:36 PM	File folder
Microsoft.AccountsControl_cw5n1h2txyewy	8/13/2016 9:36 PM	File folder
Microsoft.BioEnrollment_cw5n1h2txyewy	8/13/2016 9:36 PM	File folder
Microsoft.LockApp_cw5n1h2txyewy.DISABLED	8/13/2016 9:36 PM	File folder
Microsoft.MicrosoftEdge_8wekyb3d8bbwe	8/13/2016 4:02 PM	File folder
Microsoft.PPIProjection_cw5n1h2txyewy	8/13/2016 9:36 PM	File folder
Microsoft.Windows.AppRep.ChxApp_cw5n1h2txyewy	8/13/2016 9:36 PM	File folder
Microsoft.Windows.CloudExperienceHost_cw5n1h2txyewy	8/13/2016 9:36 PM	File folder
Microsoft.Windows.ContentDeliveryManager_cw5n1h2txyewy	8/13/2016 9:36 PM	File folder
Microsoft.Windows.Cortana_cw5n1h2txyewy	8/13/2016 4:02 PM	File folder
Microsoft.Windows.SecondaryTileExperience_cw5n1h2txyewy	8/13/2016 9:36 PM	File folder
Microsoft.XboxGameCallableUI_cw5n1h2txyewy	8/13/2016 9:36 PM	File folder
ParentalControls_cw5n1h2txyewy	8/13/2016 9:36 PM	File folder
ShellExperienceHost_cw5n1h2txyewy	8/13/2016 9:36 PM	File folder

15 items   1 item selected

The system **Lock screen** safeguards the system before a user logs on, whereas the user **Lock screen** safeguards the logged-on user account.

4 Press **WinKey + L** and see you now bypass the **Lock screen** and go directly to the Logon screen instead

It is important to recognize that this does not disable the system **Lock screen** that appears when you start your device. That is created by a separate process which should not be disabled.

AutoPlay

Windows 10 **AutoPlay** attempts to be helpful by providing related options that the user may not readily know how to access. Whenever removable media (DVDs, external hard drives, USB flash drives, etc.) are connected to the PC, a dialog box opens offering options that Windows thinks is relevant to the content on the media.

Many users, however, have no need for **AutoPlay** and find it is more of a nuisance than anything else. It can be disabled, or modified, as follows:

AutoPlay has long been regarded as an unsecure feature that provides an entry point for viruses. The version supplied with Windows 10 is much more secure.

1 Go to **Control Panel** > **AutoPlay**

2 To disable **AutoPlay** completely, uncheck the option to **Use AutoPlay for all media and devices**

You can modify **AutoPlay** for different media by choosing from the drop-down menus.

AutoPlay   — □ ×

← → ∨ ↑ 📁 > Control Panel > All Control Panel Items > AutoPlay   ∨ ↻   Search Control Panel 🔍

Choose what happens when you insert each type of media or device   ❓

☑ Use AutoPlay for all media and devices

Removable drives

💾 Removable drive   Choose a default ∨

☐ Choose what to do with each type of media

🖼 Pictures   Choose a default ∨

🎞 Videos   Choose a default ∨

🎵 Music   Choose a default ∨

🗂 Mixed content   Choose a default ∨

Camera storage

📷 Memory card   Choose a default ∨

DVDs

📀 DVD movie   Choose a default ∨

📀 Enhanced DVD movie   Choose a default ∨

⚪ Blank DVD   Choose a default ∨

📀 DVD-Audio   Choose a default ∨

Blu-ray discs

📀 Blu-ray disc movie   Choose a default ∨

⚪ Blank Blu-ray disc   Choose a default ∨

Save   Cancel

You can also completely turn off **AutoPlay** without individual media options from **Settings** > **Devices** > **AutoPlay**.

3 Click the **Save** button to implement the change, then insert some media to see **AutoPlay** now does not appear

OneDrive

The **OneDrive** cloud-based storage facility is heavily integrated into Windows 10, as Microsoft believes it is important to synchronize users' data and media across all their devices. By default, the **OneDrive** app is set to start when you sign in to Windows 10. This ensures that all the content within each folder you choose to sync on your PC is automatically kept in sync with your online **OneDrive** account.

Although **OneDrive** is regarded by many as a very useful facility, some users may not wish to use this feature. It can be disabled, or modified, as follows:

1 Go to the Taskbar **System Tray** and right-click on the **OneDrive** icon

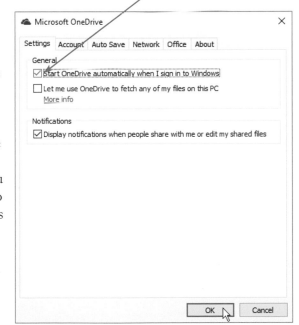

2 Choose the **Settings** item to open the **Microsoft OneDrive** dialog box

3 On the **Settings** tab, uncheck the option to **Start OneDrive automatically when I sign in to Windows**

4 Click **OK** to make the change – your files will no longer be synced when you sign in to Windows

If the **OneDrive** icon is hidden in the System Tray, go to **Settings > Personalization > Taskbar** then under Notifications click the **Select which icons appear on the Taskbar** link and slide **On** the **Microsoft OneDrive** toggle button.

The **OneDrive** icon will no longer appear in the System Tray if **OneDrive** is not running.

If you choose not to start **OneDrive** automatically when you sign in to Windows, you can start it manually at any time by clicking **Start > All apps > OneDrive**.

Only set your PC to automatically sign in if you are absolutely the only user of the PC.

You can also specify a sign-in option to resume your PC from sleep at **Settings** > **Accounts** > **Sign-in options**.

The password boxes cannot be left blank for this technique to work.

Logon Password

By default, every time a Windows 10 PC is started, a password has to be entered before the Start screen opens. However, for the many users who don't require the security provided by password protection, not only is this a nuisance, it also slows down the Startup procedure unnecessarily.

To get rid of the requirement to log on:

1 Press **WinKey + R**, to open the Run box, then enter "netplwiz" – to open the **User Accounts** dialog box

2 Uncheck the option **Users must enter a user name and password to use this computer**

3 Click **Apply** to make the change

User Accounts   ✕

Users   Advanced

Use the list below to grant or deny users access to your computer, and to change passwords and other settings.

☐ Users must enter a user name and password to use this computer.

Users for this computer:

User Name	Group
Joanne	HomeUsers; Users
Richard	HomeUsers; Users

Add...   Remove   Properties

Password for Joanne

To change the password for Joanne, click Reset Password.

Reset Password...

OK   Cancel   Apply

4 Select your user name and enter the current password (twice) – then click **OK**

5 Restart your PC to see that you no longer need to type in your password

Automatically sign in   ✕

You can set up your computer so that users do not have to type a user name and password to sign in. To do this, specify a user that will be automatically signed in below:

User name:	Joanne
Password:	••••••
Confirm Password:	••••••

OK   Cancel

6 Customization

There are many ways
to change the default
appearance of Windows 10
to personalize the PC.
This chapter shows you the
common ones, plus others
that are less well known.

The Windows Interface

Customizing the appearance of Windows allows you to create a computing environment in which you feel comfortable. You can choose your personal preferences by altering **Background, Colors, Lock screen, Account picture, Resolution, Text** and **Icon** size:

Background

 Go to **Settings** > **Personalization** then click **Background** in the left-hand pane

 Next, click the top drop-down box and choose from the **Picture, Solid color**, or **Slideshow** options

 The options below change according to your selection, so you can select a **Background** picture, color or album

84

Settings	− □ ×
⚙ Home	Preview
Find a setting 🔍	
Personalization	
🖼 Background	
🎨 Colors	
🖵 Lock screen	Background
🖉 Themes	Solid color ⌄
🖳 Start	Background colors
🖵 Taskbar	

The **Preview** area instantly changes to let you see how your selection will look, such as the gray **Solid color** background above.

Colors

You can choose to complement your background selection with an accent color for **Start menu** and window items:

 Go to **Settings** > **Personalization** > **Colors**, then uncheck the option to **Automatically pick an accent color from my background** and choose any color from the swatch

If you prefer, you can create your own custom accent color:

1 Press **WinKey + R**, to open the Run box, then enter "control color" to open the **Color and Appearance** dialog

2 Expand **Show color mixer**, adjust the sliders to mix your color, then click **Save changes** to apply the accent color

Accent Color options also provide toggle buttons to **Show color on Start, taskbar, and action center** (or leave them transparent as by default) and **Show color on title bar**.

The Windows 10 Anniversary Update introduced a **Dark mode** option – you can find toggle buttons to switch between modes at the bottom of the **Accent Color** options.

Use the **High contrast** settings in **Colors** to choose contrasting colors for those users with visual impairment.

The **Windows spotlight** option will automatically download pictures for display on your Lock screen and lets you approve pictures you like.

Settings > System > Notifications & actions > Show notifications on lock screen must be turned On to see useful app statuses on a Lock screen – such as announcing when you receive an email with

.

...cont'd

Lock screen

 Go to **Settings** > **Personalization** > **Lock screen** then click the drop-down box and choose from the **Windows spotlight**, **Picture** or **Slideshow** options

 Choose to add an app status to the **Lock screen** if desired

Account picture

Go to **Settings** > **Accounts** > **Your account** then click the **Browse for one** button under Create your picture, and choose an image to represent you

Scroll down the **Your account** screen and click the **Camera** button to take a photo with your webcam if you prefer to use a personal photo for your account picture.

Resolution

 Right-click the Desktop and click **Display settings > Display > Advanced display settings**

Resolution
1366 × 768 (Recommended)
1280 × 768
1280 × 720
1280 × 600
1024 × 768
800 × 600

If the resolution is too high, the **Desktop** won't fill the screen and text will be too small. If the resolution is too low, the **Desktop** will be blocky.

2 Choose a size from the drop-down box, then click **Apply**

Text size

1 Right-click the Desktop and choose **Display settings > Display**, then move the **Change the size of text, apps, and other items** slider

Change the size of 125% ps, and other items: 100% (Recommended)

For finer text adjustment try **Display settings > Display > Advanced display settings > Advanced sizing of text and other items**.

2 Click the **Apply** button and sign out, then sign back in

Icon size

 Right-click the Desktop then click **View** and choose **Large icons**, **Medium icons** or **Small icons**

View	>	Large icons
Sort by	>	• Medium icons
Refresh		Small icons
Paste		Auto arrange icons
Paste shortcut		✓ Align icons to grid
Undo Delete	Ctrl+Z	
		✓ Show desktop icons
New	>	
🖵 Display settings		
🖳 Personalize		

To quickly change the icon size more precisely, hold down the **Ctrl** key then scroll the mouse wheel forward and back.

87

Create Your Own Theme

Getting Windows looking just the way you want it to can take some time. Unfortunately, if you subsequently change it, either by accident or design, you may never be able to recreate it exactly. There is, however, an easy way around this. Once you have chosen your background, colors, etc., Windows allows you to save your preferred settings as a **Theme** – so you can get them back with a single mouse click:

You can create and save any number of themes.

Select the **Windows 10** theme to use the images provided with your operating system.

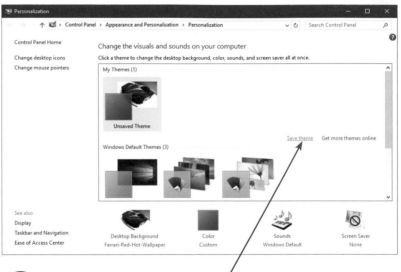

 1 Go to **Settings > Personalization > Themes > Theme settings**, then click the **Save theme** link

 2 Give your theme a name, then click **Save**

To create a shared theme, simply right-click a theme and then click **Save theme for sharing**. The theme will be saved with a **.themepack** file format that can be applied on another computer running Windows 10.

At the top of the **Personalization** utility window, under **My Themes**, your new theme will be listed. Just click to select it. Another option provided by Windows enables you to share the themes you create, or use those created by others. For example, a theme can be uploaded to a website, from where it can be downloaded by other users. Or you can save it on removable media to load onto another PC.

Get More Windows Themes

Windows 10 includes little in the way of themes, but you can easily download more free themes from Microsoft:

1 Go to **Settings** > **Personalization** > **Themes** > **Theme settings**, then click the **Get more themes online** link (see the first image opposite)

2 A selection of themes will appear in Microsoft Edge. Choose a category from the left-hand pane, then select a theme and click its **Download** button

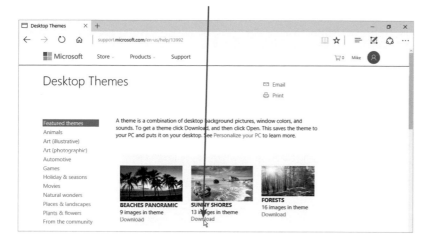

3 Click **Save**, to download the "themepack" file, then click **Open** – to add the theme to your **My Themes** collection

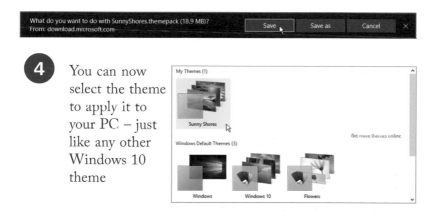

4 You can now select the theme to apply it to your PC – just like any other Windows 10 theme

An online search will reveal a virtually limitless number of themes, or "skins" as they are often called, available for download.

If you're interested in themes, visit **wincustomize.com** to find hundreds of categorized themes for Windows.

Some of the themes available on the internet can contain bugs and thus cause instability problems on the PC.

The Taskbar

The Taskbar is a highly configurable part of Windows, and setting it up to suit your method of working is important. There are quite a few adjustments you can make here that are not obvious at first glance.

Taskbar size and position

The first thing you might want to change is the size of the Taskbar. The default setting looks like this:

By right-clicking the Taskbar and selecting **Settings**, you will see that there is a **Use small taskbar buttons** toggle button. Change this to **On** to decrease the height of the Taskbar, as shown below:

You can also resize the Taskbar to any height you require by right-clicking and de-selecting **Lock the taskbar**. Then, hold the cursor over the top edge of the Taskbar and you will be able to drag it to the height you want. Then re-lock it. However, this can look a bit odd as the icons are placed at the top, as shown below:

You can get around this by docking the Taskbar at the right or left of the screen. Here, we see it docked at the right. Do this by unlocking it and simply dragging it to the required location. Increasing the size of the Taskbar and having it docked at the side of the screen is an ideal way of making use of the extra screen real-estate provided by modern wide-screen monitors.

Hot tip

If you want to change the order of a Taskbar icon, simply drag it to the required position. This also applies to icons in the notification area.

90

Hot tip

Right-click a Taskbar icon to reveal a jump list of recent files associated with the application.

Hot tip

You can also access a Taskbar icon jump list by left-clicking an icon and dragging upwards at the same time.

If you need as much screen space as possible, you can also auto-hide the Taskbar so that it releases the space it occupies when not being accessed. Do this by right-clicking the Taskbar and selecting **Settings**. Then change the **Automatically hide the taskbar in desktop mode** toggle button to **On** to implement the change.

The Taskbar location can also be set using the **Taskbar location on screen** drop-down menu in the Taskbar Settings.

While you have the **Taskbar** Settings dialog open, you can also set how icons are displayed on the Taskbar. The default **Combine taskbar buttons** setting is **Always, hide labels** whereby files of the same type are all represented by one Taskbar icon.

You can select the **When taskbar is full** combine option if you are working with lots of open files.

Hovering the cursor over the icon reveals a thumbnail of each file. One advantage of this is that all the files can be closed with one click.

If you choose the **Never** combine option, grouping is turned off and all files will have an individual Taskbar icon. The icons will also be larger, which can be useful for some users. The disadvantage is that each file has to be closed individually.

Use the **Never** combine option to always see the file name of the open file on the Taskbar icon.

System Icons

Windows comes with a default set of system icons. These won't be to everyone's tastes though, so fortunately it's an easy task to change them to something more to your liking. To change the icon of a system folder, such as **This PC** or the **Recycle Bin**, you first have to create a shortcut to it. To demonstrate this, we will change the icon for the **Recycle Bin**:

Hot tip

If you can't find an icon that appeals, you can find thousands more available on the internet.

1 Right-click the **Recycle Bin** icon and click **Create shortcut** to create a shortcut on the Desktop displaying the regular icon

2 Right-click the shortcut, click **Properties** and then **Change Icon**. This will open an icon folder

Don't forget

To associate downloaded icons with a program, in Step 3 use the **Browse** button to find and select the icon.

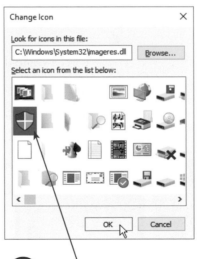

3 Select your preferred replacement icon and click **OK** to close the Change Icon dialog

4 Now, click **Apply** to implement the change, and click **OK** to close the properties dialog

Hot tip

If you would like to create your own icons check out the IcoFX icon editor at **icofx.ro**

Now, you can delete the original **Recycle Bin** icon. This procedure will work with most system folders. It will also work with third-party applications, most of which come with an icon folder of their own (these open instead of the icon folder shown above).

92

Folder Icons

Apart from changing icons for system folders and third-party applications, Windows allows you to change (and also customize) individual folder icons.

Do this as follows:

 Right-click inside the folder you want to customize and then click **Customize this folder**

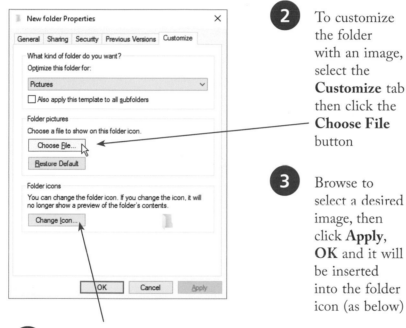

 To customize the folder with an image, select the **Customize** tab then click the **Choose File** button

 Browse to select a desired image, then click **Apply**, **OK** and it will be inserted into the folder icon (as below)

To change the folder's icon, click the **Change Icon** button, then browse to an icon folder and choose an icon

If you place a folder customized in this way on the Desktop, you may need to select a larger icon size to see the picture appear.

Using pictures is a useful way of personalizing folders, and also provides another method of readily identifying their contents.

Picture icons are an alternative way of identifying the contents of a folder.

You may need to select a larger icon size in order to see the image placed in a folder.

Click the **Restore Default** button on the **Customize** tab to stop using the inserted image on the folder.

Display a Logon Message

In certain situations it can be useful to greet users of a computer with a message when they log on. This might be something friendly, or a warning of some description. An example of the latter could occur in an office environment where company email and internet facilities might be misused by employees:

1 Open the Registry Editor and locate the following key: **HKEY_LOCAL_MACHINE\SOFTWARE\ Microsoft\Windows NT\CurrentVersion\Winlogon**

Hot tip

Press **WinKey + R** then type "regedit" in the Run box to open the **Registry Editor**.

Name	Type	Data
LegalNoticeCaption	REG_SZ	
LegalNoticeText	REG_SZ	
PasswordExpiryWarning	REG_DWORD	0x00000005 (5)

Computer\HKEY_LOCAL_MACHINE\SOFTWARE\Microsoft\Windows NT\CurrentVersion\Winlogon

2 Double-click the **LegalNoticeCaption** key. In the **Value Data** box, type your caption, e.g. "ATTENTION" and click OK

Edit String

Value name: LegalNoticeCaption

Value data: ATTENTION

Beware

Click **File** > **Export** to back up the Registry before making changes. Click **File** > **Import** to restore from a backup.

3 Now, click the **LegalNoticeText** key and type a message in the **Value Data** box

Edit String

Value name: LegalNoticeText

Value data: This PC is being monitored by the System Administration Team

4 Click OK, restart the computer and your captioned message will be displayed immediately before the **Logon screen** appears

Don't forget

This feature is really intended for system administrators. However, you may find a use for it.

ATTENTION
This PC is being monitored by the System Administration Team

OK

7 Paranoia

This chapter looks at the ways users unwittingly reveal what they've been doing on the PC, and shows how to avoid this. We also look at privacy and security on the PC and the internet.

Keep Your Activities Private

It's not easy to use a computer without leaving traces of what you have been doing. Windows keeps records of user activity in several places, and anyone who knows where to look can find out what websites you've visited, files you've accessed, programs you've been using, etc. If you're not careful, they can even access your password-protected web pages.

The following are the most common giveaways:

Jump Lists

When you right-click a program's icon on the Taskbar, a **Jump List** of files recently opened with that program will be revealed, as shown below:

If you have been using Microsoft Word to type a letter to your Bank Manager, for example, a subsequent user will be able to see the name of the file in the **Jump List** and also open it, if you don't log out.

To prevent this, do the following:

1 Go to **Settings** > **Personalization** then choose the **Start** item in the left-hand pane

2 Slide the toggle button to the **Off** position to disable **Show recently opened items in Jump Lists...**

Items in **Jump Lists** can be deleted individually by right-clicking on them and then clicking **Remove from this list**.

Use this tip so you don't have to keep checking that you've cleared your Jump List history.

Note that this action will not disable the **Jump List** feature completely. It will still be there, but with no items on it.

96

...cont'd

Most Recently Used Lists (MRUs)

The most common method of preventing other users from seeing a private file is to simply squirrel it away in a location that is not likely to be accessed by someone else – out of sight, out of mind, as the saying goes.

However, while a file hidden in this way may be difficult to physically locate, there is a way for another user to easily find it.

This is courtesy of the **Most Recently Used** files feature, found in most programs, that enables a user to reopen a recent file quickly without having to go to its location.

The **Most Recently Used** list is commonly referred to by its abbreviation as **MRU** list.

So, a user looking to keep a particular file private will need to clear the **Most Recently Used** list in any program it has been accessed with recently – see Hot tip.

Windows Searches

Another method of finding data is using the Windows **Search** utility. Unless the user has set the Hidden attribute of a file (as described on page 106), if another user specifies that file type in a search, the file will be revealed (if you have not logged out, or if the documents are public or shared). For example, if someone was to type ".doc" into the Search box all Microsoft Word documents would be found. The problem here is that there is no way to configure the **Search** utility to prevent another user from searching for a file of a specific type.

With most programs, the **Most Recently Used** list can be cleared by disabling the feature. For example, in Microsoft Word 2016 (shown here) go to **File > Options > Advanced** then scroll down to the **Display** category and set **Show this number of Recent Documents** to zero.

...cont'd

So the only way to prevent files being revealed by Windows searches is to place them in a password-protected folder. Unfortunately, Windows 10 does not provide a way to password-protect individual folders. The only way to do it, therefore, is to install a third-party utility – see page 111.

Run command history

The Run command keeps a history of all entries made. This can reveal to other users what files, and even web pages, you have accessed. For example, someone typing the letter "W" into the Run box will see a list of all the web pages that have been accessed since the history folder was last cleared.

Press **WinKey + R** to open the Run box, then enter a path, URL or app command, such as:
calc (Calculator),
charmap
(Character Map),
cmd (Command Prompt),
control (Control Panel),
dxdiag
(DirectX Diagnostic Tool),
notepad (Notepad),
mspaint (Paint),
msinfo32
(System Information),
winver (About Windows),
write (WordPad).

Furthermore, by selecting an entry and clicking **OK**, the web page will be opened in the PC's web browser.

There is a Registry setting that will clear the Run history, but an easier way is to download and install the free **CCleaner** utility program from **piriform.com**
This will clear not only the Windows Run history but also the **Most Recently Used** lists of your installed program (see page 97).

The **CCleaner** utility program can also be used to clean the Registry (see page 29).

Hide Your Browsing Tracks

Browsing history

In the same way that Windows keeps records of user activity, so does the Microsoft Edge web browser.

This information is held in three categories:

- **Browsing history** – a chronological record of every website and page the user has visited.

- **Cookies and saved website data** – cookies are text files that websites download to your PC. They have several purposes; one is to identify the user should they visit that website again. Often, they will also reveal the type of website, for example with the cookie data **mike@luckydollarcasino**

- **Cached data and files** – a cache of the pages you have accessed. Should you revisit a particular web page, your browser will retrieve it from this cache rather than from the web. This makes access to the page quicker.

Don't forget to check your internet Favorites. When accessed, certain websites will automatically place a link to their website here. Common culprits in this respect are porn and gambling websites. Anyone who happens to use your browser may see anything which has been added in this way.

99

For users who wish to keep their internet activities private, Microsoft Edge provides a **Clear browsing data** utility:

1 Open Microsoft Edge, then click the **...** (**More options**) button and then **Settings**

2 Under the "Clear browsing data" heading, click the **Choose what to clear** button

3 Check the categories to be cleared, then click the **Clear** button to implement your choice

Screenshot of Microsoft Edge "Clear browsing data" panel showing:
- — ☐ ✕
- ☐ ☆ | ≡ 📝 ◌ ⋯
- « Clear browsing data 📌
- ☑ Browsing history
- ☑ Cookies and saved website data
- ☑ Cached data and files
- ☑ Download history
- ☐ Form data
- ☐ Passwords
- Show more ∨
- Clear
- Always clear this when I close the browser
- 🔘 On
- Change what Microsoft Edge knows about me in the cloud
- Clear Bing search history
- Learn more

The **Clear browsing data** utility lets you eradicate all records of your internet activities, or just some of them by checking certain items.

...cont'd

AutoComplete

Microsoft Edge has a feature called **AutoComplete** that enables the browser to automatically enter web addresses, user names, passwords and data entered on web-based forms. This can be convenient as it saves the user from having to type out this information each time.

However, it can also be dangerous, as it allows other people to access your password-protected pages and see what data you've entered into forms, etc. It will also enable any snooper to see which websites you have visited, and any keywords entered in search engine Search boxes.

If you wish to keep this type of information private, then you need to disable **AutoComplete** or alter its settings:

 Go to **Control Panel** > **Internet Options**, then click the **Content** tab

 Click the **Settings** button in the **AutoComplete** section

 Uncheck both **Address bar** and **User names and passwords on forms** options, then click **OK**

Hot tip

Enabling **AutoComplete** to remember web addresses is safe and can be very useful.

Don't forget

The safest way to use **AutoComplete** is to disable the **User names and passwords on forms** option.

Hot tip

Disabling any of the **AutoComplete** settings will also remove any information previously held regarding the setting. It won't still be there should you subsequently re-enable it.

InPrivate Browsing

As we have seen on page 99, it is possible to delete your browsing history after each session. However, there are two problems with this approach:

- You may forget to do it

- You have to delete the entire history when maybe all you want to do is to delete a small part of it – it's an all-or-nothing action

The solution is a feature in Microsoft Edge called **InPrivate Browsing**. When used, **InPrivate** temporarily suspends the browser's automatic caching functions and, at the same time, keeps your previous browsing history intact. A typical example of when you might want to do this is buying a gift online for a loved one – once done, you can revert to browsing as normal. Your browsing history up to the point of opening the **InPrivate** session is kept, but the **InPrivate** session itself is not.

To begin an **InPrivate Browsing** session:

 In Microsoft Edge click the **...** (**More options**) button on the menu bar

 Select the **New InPrivate window** option

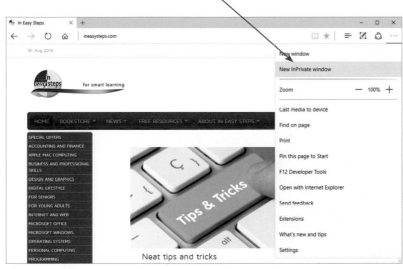

Neat tips and tricks

The **Clear browsing data** utility in **Settings** provides an option to always clear selected records of your internet activities when you close the browser.

You can also press the **Ctrl + Shift + P** keys to open a new **InPrivate** window.

While **InPrivate Browsing** keeps other people who use your computer from seeing what sites you've visited, it does not prevent someone on your network, such as a network administrator, from accessing this information.

Anonymous Browsing

Personal privacy on the internet, as any computer-savvy user knows, is becoming increasingly difficult to maintain. In many cases, the content you view actually comes from third-party sites. While most of these sites are quite legitimate, there are some which conceal scripts in their content that track your actions as you browse the internet. To help protect users against this, **Internet Explorer** supports a feature known as **Tracking Protection**. This enables you to prevent specific third-party sites from tracking your online movements.

The system works by loading a **Tracking Protection List** (TPL) of known offenders into **Internet Explorer**. As you subsequently browse the internet, Internet Explorer will prevent your data from being accessed by any of the sites specified in the TPL:

At the time of writing, **Tracking Protection List** support is not available in the Microsoft Edge web browser. Hopefully TPL support will be added later.

1 You can see the **Tracking Protection List** by clicking the ⚙ **Tools** icon at the top far-right of Internet Explorer. Then click **Manage Add-ons > Tracking Protection**

There is a **Get a Tracking Protection List online** link in the **Manage Add-ons** dialog but this will not work successfully if Microsoft Edge is set as the default web browser. You should manually enter the URL into Internet Explorer instead, as described here.

2 To add a **Tracking Protection List**, navigate Internet Explorer to **iegallery.com/en-us/trackingprotectionlists** then choose a list and click its **Add** button

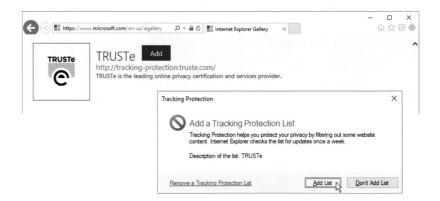

...cont'd

3 The **Tracking Protection List** will now be added to Internet Explorer. Open **Manage Add-ons** again to see the **Tracking Protection List** you have installed

Manage Add-ons			
View and manage your Internet Explorer add-ons

Add-on Types	Name	Status	Address
Toolbars and Extensions	EasyPrivacy	Enabled	http://easylist-msie.adblockplus.org/easyprivacy.tpl
Search Providers	TRUSTe	Enabled	http://easy-tracking-protection.truste.com/easy.tpl
Accelerators	Your Personalized List	Enabled	
Tracking Protection			

TRUSTe
Address: http://easy-tracking-protection.truste.com/easy.tpl
More information

Remove   Disable

Learn more about Tracking Protection   Close

You can also create a personal **Tracking Protection List** to be added to Internet Explorer:

1 In the **Manage add-ons** dialog, select the **Your Personalized List** item, then set it to **Enabled** if **Disabled**

2 Double-click the **Your Personalized List** item to see your list

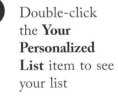

Personalized Tracking Protection List

When you visit multiple websites that contain content from the same provider, such as a map, advertisement, or web measurement tools, some information about your visits might be shared with the content provider. If you choose to block content, portions of the websites you visit might not be available.

○ Automatically block   ● Choose content to block or allow

Content provider	Status	Used by	Content
crowdscience.com	Blocked	10 sites	ping.js
statcounter.com	Blocked	10 sites	t.php
tynt.com	Blocked	10 sites	Tracer.js
tynt.com	Blocked	10 sites	p
rubiconproject.com	Blocked	10 sites	tap.php

Allow   Block

Show content from providers used by this number of websites you've visited. (3-30) [10]   Refresh

Learn more about Tracking Protection   OK   Cancel

3 If your list is empty, browse for a day or two, return to see list items and then you can select **Choose content to block or allow**

 Hot tip
Click the **Learn more about Tracking Protection** link in the **Manage Add-ons** dialog for more details.

 Don't forget
You can add as many **Tracking Protection List items** as you like.

 Beware
Internet Explorer automatically generates a **Tracking Protection List** based on the sites the user visits. This is called "Your Personalized List", and is in addition to any **Tracking Protection List** added by the user.

103

Hide Your Drives

The following procedure does more than just hide a file or folder – it actually hides the drive where the file/folder is located. For example, we can hide **Drive E** from the system shown here:

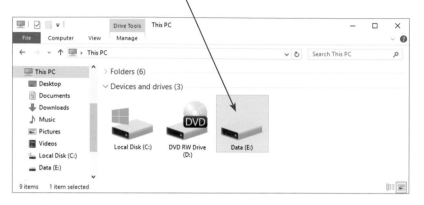

If you are going to be hiding and unhiding a drive on a regular basis, having to go into the Registry each time will be a pain. So instead, you can create a shortcut:

Create a **NoDrives** DWORD, as described, and give it a value of 0. Then, right-click the **Explorer** folder on the left and click **Export**. In the **File name** box, type: "Unhide.reg", then save it to the Desktop.

Next, go back to the **NoDrives** DWORD and in the **Value data** box enter the number of the drive to be hidden. Return to the **Explorer** folder and export it with the name "Hide.reg".

Now, just click the **Hide** icon to conceal the drive and the **Unhide** icon to reveal it (not forgetting to restart the PC).

104

1 Start the Registry Editor and locate the following key: **HKEY_CURRENT_USER\SOFTWARE\Microsoft\ Windows\CurrentVersion\Policies**

2 Right-click the **Policies** folder and click **New > Key**, then name the new key "Explorer"

3 Click the **Explorer** folder, and on the right, right-click and select **New > DWORD (32-bit) Value**, then name it "NoDrives"

4 Double-click **NoDrives** to open the Edit dialog, then choose a **Base** of **Decimal**

5 Now, in the **Value data** box, enter the number of the drive to be hidden from the values in the table below: (For example, for **Drive E** enter **16**)

Drive A – 1	Drive J – 512	Drive S – 262144
Drive B – 2	Drive K – 1024	Drive T – 524288
Drive C – 4	Drive L – 2048	Drive U – 1048576
Drive D – 8	Drive M – 4096	Drive V – 2097152
Drive E – 16	Drive N – 8192	Drive W – 4194304
Drive F – 32	Drive O – 16384	Drive X – 8388608
Drive G – 64	Drive P – 32768	Drive Y – 16777216
Drive H – 128	Drive Q – 65536	Drive Z – 33554432
Drive I – 256	Drive R – 131072	All – 67108863

The dashes in this table are not a minus sign, just enter the numeric value listed.

6 Click **OK**, then restart the PC, or sign out then back in, to implement the change

7 Open **File Explorer > This PC** then choose **Devices and drives** to see that the drive is now hidden

Decimal values are provided here but you could use their hexadecimal equivalent. For example, decimal 16 is hexadecimal 10.

To unhide a drive, return to the **NoDrives** key in the Registry Editor then enter **0** in its **Value data** box.

Hide Your Private Files

Users who want to hide a file or folder quickly can do so by means of the Windows **Hidden Files and Folders** feature. While this is intended primarily to conceal important system files, which if modified or deleted can cause damage to the operating system, it can also be used to hide other files or folders.

 Right-click the file to be hidden and click **Properties**

Hot tip

Another way to hide a folder is to squirrel it away in a folder containing a mass of other folders – just don't forget where you put it.

Don't forget

In **File Explorer** you can check the **Hidden items** option on the **View** tab to see any hidden files.

 On the **General** tab, check the **Hidden** box in the **Attributes** section

 Click the **Apply** button and the file icon will disappear

To unhide the file, go to **File Explorer Options** > **Control Panel**. Click the **View** tab, and check **Show hidden files, folders, and drives**

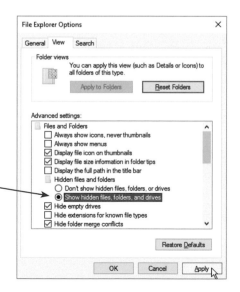

Click the **Apply** button and the file icon will reappear

Beware

The method described on this page, while useful, is by no means secure. Anyone who knows about this feature will be able to access anything you hide in this way.

8 Security

Secure Your PC Physically

One of the most glaring security loopholes of all is physical theft. The PC's data may be well secured but what's to prevent someone from simply tucking the system case under their arm and walking away with it. They may not be able to access the data on the PC but you've still lost it.

While your home insurance (if you have it – many don't, and assuming it pays out) will cover the cost of replacing the PC, it won't replace your data.

So if yours is irreplaceable, and you are not in the habit of creating up-to-date backups on separate media (writable discs, USB flash drives, etc), or cannot afford to be without the PC for the length of time needed to replace it, then you need to physically secure it.

The following methods are available:

Alarms

These are the least effective method as they don't provide any physical restraint, but may be sufficient to deter the casual thief. A typical system will consist of a motion sensor that you fix to the system case. If someone tries to open the case or pick it up, an alarm will be triggered.

Cables

A cable system consists of plates, which are fixed to the case and peripherals by bolts or industrial-strength adhesive. The cable is fixed to one plate, looped through the others and then fixed to an anchor plate on the desk. To steal the PC, the thief will have to steal the desk along with it. They can, however, open the case and steal all the components inside.

Enclosures

These are lockable heavy-duty metal boxes into which the system case is placed, and are secured to the desk by bolts or adhesive. This is the best method, as not only is it impossible to steal the PC, it is also impossible to open the case and steal the PC's components.

So, if you want to keep both the PC and the data it contains safe, take steps to physically secure it.

Hot tip

Most laptops provide a connector to which a cable can be connected to secure them.

Don't forget

Locking devices for removable media drives are also available. These are mounted on the front panel of the drive and prevent access to it.

Restrict Access to Windows

The next step is to prevent access to the operating system. Here are three ways to do this:

Set a Boot password

Most BIOS setup programs provide an option to password-protect the bootup procedure. To do this, start the PC and enter the BIOS setup program – see page 125.

On the opening screen you should see an option to "Set User Password". Select this and enter a password – this password-protects the BIOS setup program. Then, look for a security option (usually found in the Advanced BIOS Features page). This enables you to set a boot password. Do so, save the changes and exit the BIOS. Now bootup will stop at the boot screen and ask you to enter the password.

Set a Logon password

During the installation routine of Windows 10, the user is asked to specify a password. However, this is only mandatory if using a Microsoft Account – if you set up Windows using a Local Account, a password is not necessary.

If the latter option was taken when the PC was set up, you can set a password now, as described below:

1 Go to **Settings** > **Accounts**, then click **Sign-in options**

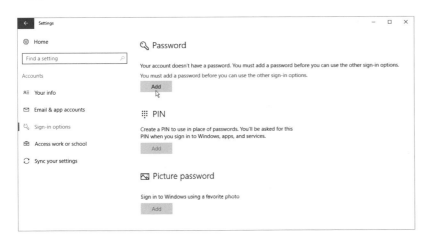

2 Under **Password**, click the **Add** button, then follow the prompts to create a Logon password

Password-protecting the BIOS setup program as well means a hacker has two passwords to crack before the PC can be booted up.

If you choose not to log on with a Microsoft Account, some features of Windows 10 will be unavailable to you.

109

You may choose to log on to Windows 10 with a regular password, a PIN, or a picture password.

...cont'd

Create an encrypted password disk

This is an extremely secure method of securing a PC by using an encrypted key. Read the Beware tip before you get started.

WARNING: This procedure cannot be undone. Be quite sure that you need this level of security before you start.

1 Open Run by pressing **WinKey + R**, then enter "syskey" in the box and press **Enter**

2 In the dialog box that opens, click the **Update** button

3 Check **System Generated Password** and then **Store Startup Key on Floppy Disk**

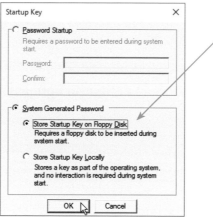

4 Click **OK**, then insert a floppy disk (see Beware tip) when prompted. An encrypted key will be saved onto the disk

5 From this point on, every time you boot the PC, it will be necessary to insert the disk into the floppy drive before you can access the Logon screen – be sure you don't lose it, otherwise you won't be able to access your own computer

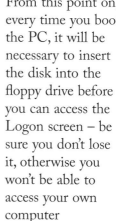

The **syskey** utility requires a floppy disk as the storage medium. However, very few PCs use floppy drives these days, so a better option is to use a USB flash drive. This will need to be configured to use the **A:** drive letter commonly assigned to the floppy drive.

This can be done in **Windows Drive Management**, which is located in the Control Panel. Click **Administrative Tools** > **Computer Management** > **Disk Management**. Right-click the USB drive and select **Change drive letter and paths...**

Note that if the **A:** drive letter is not available, you will need to disable the floppy drive in the PC's BIOS.

110

Password-Protect Folders

With access to both the PC and the operating system secured, the really security-conscious user may want to make things even more difficult for a potential intruder. The way to do this is to password-protect any sensitive data so that even if someone does manage to gain entry to the PC, they can't get to your data.

Unfortunately, Windows 10 doesn't provide a folder/file password-protection function. The only option, therefore, is to use a third-party application. Do an online search and you will find dozens of programs of this type. A typical example is one called **Folder Password Protect**, which is available from **protect-folders.com**

This simple but effective application lets you password-protect any number of folders, either individually or collectively, by adding them to a main window, as shown below:

1 Click the **Add** button and choose one or more folders to be protected, then click **Next** to open a password request dialog

2 Enter the desired password then click **OK** and you're done – the selected folder, or folders, are protected

Folder Password Protect

Select Folders to Lock

Click the Add button to include your folders in the list of folders to protect.

C:\Users\mike_\Documents\Banking Data

<< Add...
>> Remove

About... | Help... | < Back | Next > | Exit

3 To unprotect a folder, select it and enter the password. It couldn't be simpler

Folder Password Protect

Enter the Password

Your password: ●●●●●●●●●●●●●

Did you forget your password? Click the Get a Hint button. | Get a hint...

About... | Help... | < Back | Next > | Exit

A badly-written password-protection utility can be more dangerous than not having one at all. If it contains bugs, you could end up losing your passwords and thus your data. For this reason, give freeware and shareware programs a definite miss.

Choose a password you can easily remember, so you need never write it down. Choose a password you can type quickly, so it can't be discovered by someone looking over your shoulder.

Keep Your Passwords Safe

Most computer users these days will have several passwords – many will have a dozen or more. It can be difficult to remember these passwords, particularly those that are rarely used. Accordingly, many users keep a file on the PC that contains all their passwords.

However, while this ensures they don't forget them, a new problem arises – password theft. Unfortunately, Windows does not provide a utility that can be used to safely store and manage passwords.

So what we suggest is that you acquire a password manager program. The easiest way is to download one from the internet – you will find literally hundreds, some free, some not. The one shown below, **Dashlane**, is a typical example.

These programs work by hiding the passwords behind asterisks; a mouse click is required to reveal them. Thus, malicious software will not be able to see what they are. The password managers themselves are also password-protected to prevent physical access by a snooper. So all you have to do is remember a single password.

The **Dashlane** password manager is available free online for download from **dashlane.com**

Don't forget

A password manager will need you to supply a "master password", which you must remember to keep safe.

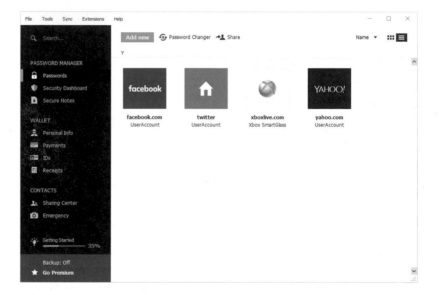

Hot tip

The **RoboForm** password manager is available free online for download from **roboform.com**

Good password managers have an auto-fill facility, similar to Microsoft Edge's **AutoComplete**. It should also be possible to install and run them from removable media. A good example is **RoboForm**, which can be used from a flash drive.

Encrypt Your Private Data

We've seen how to secure your data by password-protecting both it and the PC. What we haven't considered yet is the possibility of someone cracking your password. The answer to this is to encrypt the data itself, thus adding a further layer of protection.

Windows 10 provides data encryption via its **Encrypting File System (EFS)** feature and it's very easy to use. Simply right-click the folder containing files to be encrypted and click **Properties**. Then, click the **Advanced** button and in the dialog box that opens, select **Encrypt contents to secure data**. When the encryption has finished, the names of the encrypted files will change to green, signifying that they are encrypted.

However, even though it is encrypted, the data is still vulnerable to someone who either physically steals the entire PC, or the drive the data is stored on. This is due to the fact that EFS only works on drives formatted with the NTFS file system, so if the encrypted folder is copied to a non-NTFS drive, the encryption is removed and the data will thus be accessible.

NTFS (New Technology File System) is the file system used by the Windows 10 operating system.

To guard against this, you need to use another feature provided by Windows 10. This is called **BitLocker Drive Encryption** and it provides offline data protection by making it possible to encrypt an entire drive (including removable USB flash drives).

Go to **Control Panel** and click **BitLocker Drive Encryption**. Click **Turn on BitLocker** next to the drive to be encrypted and then follow the prompts – this will include setting a password to unlock the drive. Note that the encryption process can take a very long time. When it is finished, if you go to **This PC**, you will see that the encrypted drive now has a padlocked drive icon.

BitLocker Encryption is only available in the Pro and Enterprise versions of Windows 10.

If you remove the drive and then reinstall it, a dialog box will pop up asking for the password, as shown on the left.

To remove encryption or set a different method of unlocking the drive, re-open the utility and select **Turn off BitLocker**.

BitLocker (E:)

Enter password to unlock this drive.

••••••••

More options

Unlock

Note that **BitLocker** cannot be used on a single file or folder. You have to encrypt the entire drive that contains the data to be protected.

Data Backup

Don't forget

For those of you not up to speed with current computer terminology, "The Cloud" or "Cloud computing" is a term for the delivery of hosted services over the internet. On this page it refers to the use of the free storage space provided by Microsoft, which users can use to safely store their data via the **OneDrive** app.

Another way in which your data can be compromised is losing it. This can be accidental deletion, a virus attack, hardware or operating system failure, or data corruption. As a safeguard against any of these potential threats, you need to create a backup on a separate medium. Traditionally, this has required a backup program, and Windows 8 provided an excellent imaging utility that was called Windows 7 File Recovery. However, in Windows 10 it has been removed because Microsoft is promoting the Cloud as a backup medium, via its **OneDrive** app. Therefore, anyone wishing to do image or large-scale backups in Windows 10 will have to purchase a third-party utility. There are many good choices here, such as **Acronis True Image**. This offers image backups, continuous backups in real time, plus a host of other features.

Windows itself offers just two methods of data backup: File History, which we look at on page 115, and the aforementioned **OneDrive** app. The latter is deeply integrated into Windows 10, which makes it very straightforward to use. For example, when you save a document with the **Save As** command, the first option you see is **OneDrive**. Select this, and the file will be seamlessly uploaded to your **OneDrive** account, where it will be safe from whatever disaster may befall your PC. Furthermore, by default, your **Documents** folder is synced to your online **OneDrive** account. So files can be automatically backed up simply by placing them in the **Documents** folder. Thus, **OneDrive** provides an ideal method of backing up small files. The drawback is that the total amount of free storage is currently restricted to just 5GB, but you can buy an upgrade to 50GB, and an **Office 365** subscription includes a whopping 1TB of OneDrive storage.

Hot tip

A big advantage of using **OneDrive** to back up your data is that once configured, the process is automatic – you'll never forget to do it.

Right-click the **OneDrive** icon in the System Tray, then choose **Settings**. Now, select the **Account** tab and click **Choose folders** to configure the folders you want to sync.

Microsoft OneDrive	✕
Sync your OneDrive files to this PC	
The files you sync will take up space on this PC	
☑ Sync all files and folders in my OneDrive	
Sync only these folders	
☑ Files not in a folder (1.9 MB)	
☑ Documents (1.2 MB)	
☑ Email attachments (402.0 KB)	
☑ Favourites (1.5 KB)	
☑ Music (6.2 MB)	
☑ Pictures (3.9 MB)	
☑ Projects (3.3 MB)	
Selected: 16.8 MB	
Remaining space on C: 160.6 GB	
	OK Cancel

Recover Your Data

File History is a replacement for the "Previous Versions" utility found in Windows 7, which allows users to quickly restore individual files that have been modified, damaged or even deleted.

It works by making automatic backups (every hour by default) of all files stored in the following folders: **Contacts**, **Desktop**, **Favorites**, and **Libraries**. All other folders are ignored. However, if you want to include a folder other than the default ones, all you have to do is place it in a library.

By default, **File History** is turned off. Enable it as follows:

1 Connect an external drive to the PC. Typically, this will be a USB flash drive or external hard drive

2 Go to **Control Panel** > **File History**. Assuming you have correctly connected an external drive, you will see this:

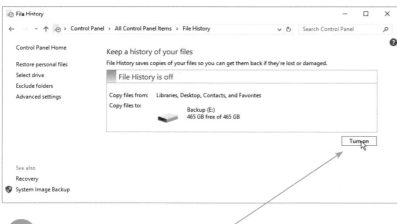

3 Now, click the **Turn on** button

All files in the above-mentioned folders will now be automatically backed up every hour. Existing backups are not over-written by new ones – each backup is kept, so over a period of time a file history is created. This enables a file to be restored from a backup created at a specific hour and day.

To restore a file, click the **Restore personal files** link at the top-left of the window. Then, browse to the required backup.

The only way to specify additional folders to be backed up is to add them to a library.

You can choose specific folders not to back up in **File History** by clicking the **Exclude folders** link.

By default, backups are made every hour. However, this can be changed by clicking **Advanced settings** and choosing a different interval, from **Every 10 minutes** to **Daily**.

Keep Windows Updated

While Windows 10 is currently a very secure operating system, rest assured that even as you read this, many people are working on ways to circumvent its security features, as they did (successfully) with previous versions of Windows. To counter this, Microsoft releases a stream of automatic updates for Windows 10, which plug security loopholes as and when they are discovered.

If you have other Microsoft products installed it is convenient to also allow automatic updates for these, and you may additionally enable faster updates for all PCs on your local network:

Hot tip

If you are concerned that automatic updates will slow your internet connection, you needn't be. The utility uses unused internet bandwidth to "trickle-feed" the updates download without affecting the user's browsing activities.

1 Go to **Settings**, **Update & security**, **Advanced options**, then check the option to **Give me updates for other Microsoft products when I update Windows**

← Settings	— □ ×

⚙ Advanced options

Choose how updates are installed

☑ Give me updates for other Microsoft products when I update Windows.

☐ Use my sign in info to automatically finish setting up my device after an update.
Learn more

Privacy statement

Choose how updates are delivered

2 Next, click **Choose how updates are delivered** and turn **On** the **Updates from more than one place** option, then select **PCs on my local network**

Windows Update Delivery Optimization is new in Windows 10. It helps you get updates more quickly and sends updates to other PCs on your network. Although the Delivery Optimization files are sizeable you may not want to delete them – see page 31.

← Settings	— □ ×

⚙ Choose how updates are delivered

Updates from more than one place

Download Windows updates and apps from other PCs in addition to Microsoft. This can help speed up app and update downloads.
Learn more

When this is turned on, your PC may also send parts of previously downloaded Windows updates and apps to PCs on your local network, or PCs on the Internet, depending on what's selected below.

◯▬ On

Get updates from Microsoft, and get updates from and send updates to

◉ PCs on my local network

◯ PCs on my local network, and PCs on the Internet

Computer Quick Lock

Another way in which the security of your PC can be compromised is by a casual snooper. They may, actually, not be snooping at all – it could be a family member who sits down at the PC while you've popped out to a different room.

One way to prevent this is to log off. However, doing this will close all your running applications so you will have to restart them all when you log back on.

A much quicker way is to create a shortcut on the Desktop or Taskbar that will enable you to lock the PC instantly, should it ever be necessary to do so.

To do this:

The account must be password-protected before it can be locked.

1 Right-click the Desktop and select **New** > **Shortcut**. In the **Type the location of the item** box, precisely enter: **rundll32.exe user32.dll,LockWorkStation**

Be aware that there is a space between **.exe** and **user**. The text must be entered correctly for the shortcut to work.

←   ⬚   Create Shortcut   ✕

What item would you like to create a shortcut for?

This wizard helps you to create shortcuts to local or network programs, files, folders, computers, or Internet addresses.

Type the location of the item:

`rundll32.exe user32.dll,LockWorkStation`   Browse...

Click Next to continue.

Next   Cancel

---

 2 Click **Next** and then give the shortcut a suitable name, e.g. "Lock PC"

If you don't like the look of the shortcut icon, you can change it to something more to your liking – as described on page 92.

The shortcut icon will now appear on the Desktop, from where it can be easily accessed to quickly lock your PC. Alternatively, you can drag the shortcut to the Taskbar if you prefer it there.

Security on the Internet

The source of most dangers to PC owners is the internet. Having learned from its mistakes with early versions of Internet Explorer, Microsoft has improved the security of the Microsoft Edge web browser. Here, we'll look at a couple of issues regarding internet security and Windows 10.

The first concerns Windows 10's anti-malware utility, **Windows Defender**. If you open this in the **Control Panel**, you'll see it's configured to do a **Quick scan**. We suggest you change this to a **Full scan**. Then, check that the utility's spyware and virus definitions are up-to-date; if not, click the **Update** tab.

The second concerns the **Enhanced Protected Mode** feature which is enabled by default in Microsoft Edge. Briefly, in **Enhanced Protected Mode**, Microsoft Edge cannot modify user or system files and settings without user consent. **Enhanced Protected Mode** requires the user to confirm any activity that tries to download something to the PC or start another program. By ensuring the user consents to these kinds of actions, the likelihood of automated and/or unwanted software installation is reduced. This feature also makes you aware of what a website is trying to do, thus giving you a chance to stop it.

However, **Enhanced Protected Mode** is not enabled by default with Internet Explorer, and users are advised to enable it as follows:

A virus "definition" (a.k.a. virus signature) is the unique binary pattern that identifies a computer virus.

It is essential that **Windows Defender** is kept updated with the latest virus definitions in order to protect the PC.

118

When browsing with **Microsoft Edge**, you can click the **...** (More Options) button then choose **Open with Internet Explorer** to see enabled **Enhanced Protection Mode** request confirmation before downloading an item to your PC.

1 Go to **Control Panel > Internet Options** then choose the **Advanced** tab

2 Check **Enable Enhanced Protected Mode**, then click the **Apply** button and restart your PC

Privacy Issues with Sync

A feature in Windows 10, and one that is sure to be popular with many users, is **Sync**. This enables settings and data to be synchronized across a number of Windows 10 devices. For example, you may have a Windows 10 PC on which you keep Contact and Email Account details. By using the same Microsoft Account on your Windows 10 cellphone, this data will be automatically copied to your phone. Also, any subsequent changes to the data will be updated automatically, i.e. synchronized.

While this is undoubtedly convenient and will prove to be a real timesaver for many users, there are sure to be occasions when it is not desirable from a security point of view. For instance, if several people have access to one of your devices, you may not want your website passwords synced. Another scenario is your **Personalization** settings, which, by default, will be synced and applied to all of your Windows 10 devices – this is something you may not want.

The solution is to configure the **Sync** feature to disregard settings you'd rather not share across your devices. Do it as follows:

1 Go to **Settings** > **Accounts**, then choose **Sync your settings** in the left-hand pane

Full synchronization allows your documents, photos, music, etc. to be accessible on all devices logged on with the same Microsoft Account.

Synchronization lets your background, color, etc. settings be replicated across your devices.

119

Settings		
← Settings	— □ ×	
⚙ Home	**Sync settings**	
Find a setting 🔍	🔘 On	
Accounts	**Individual sync settings**	
R≡ Your info	**Theme**	
✉ Email & app accounts	🔘 On	
🔍 Sign-in options	**Internet Explorer settings**	
🗂 Access work or school	🔘 On	
🗛 Family & other people	**Passwords**	
↻ Sync your settings	🔘 On	
	Language preferences	
	🔘 On	
	Ease of Access	
	🔘 On	
	Other Windows settings	
	🔘 On	

Slide the **Sync settings** toggle button to **Off** if you want to stop all synchronization.

2 You will now see options for turning off **Individual sync settings** (synchronization) for various features

Child Protection Utilities

The internet is a minefield that can expose naïve and trusting kids to many different types of threat. All responsible parents will want to minimize, if not eliminate completely, the risks to which their children are exposed. There are many commercially-available programs that help them to do this, such as **Net Nanny**, **CyberPatrol**, etc. The best of these applications enable parents to control and monitor every aspect of what the typical child might want to do on a computer and the internet. Windows 10 provides its own inbuilt utility – **Family Safety**.

Hot tip

By itself, the **Family Safety** utility does not offer much to get excited about. However, when used in conjunction with the **Family Safety** website (see next page), you can control pretty much anything your kids do, not only on the internet but also on the PC itself.

1 Go **Settings > Accounts > Family & other people**, then sign in with a Microsoft Account and click **Add a family member**. In the dialog box that opens, you will be prompted to **Add a child or an adult?**

2 Click **Add a child** and **The person I want to add doesn't have an email address**, then click **Next** and enter their personal details

3 Return to **Settings > Accounts** to see the new child account has been added. Click **Manage family settings online** to edit the settings

Beware

Before the child account is added to your family settings, the child may need to respond to an email invitation or log on to a Windows 10 device for verification.

...cont'd

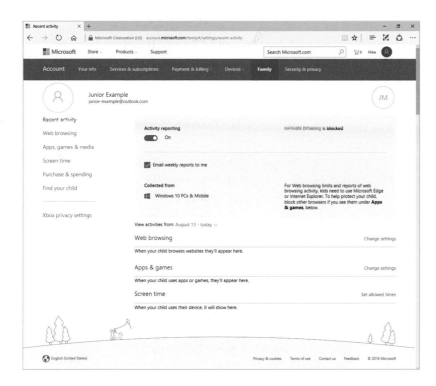

Hot tip

Adjust the **Screen time** settings to limit the times of day, and how much time the child can spend on their screen per day.

This provides a web-based control panel (shown above) from which you can do the following:

- Block/allow specific websites.

- Use web filtering to block unsuitable content. Different filters can be created for each child.

- Block file downloads.

- Control and monitor who your kids are communicating with via instant messaging software and email.

- Get monitoring reports on what your kids have been doing, both on the internet and the PC.

- Access and adjust each child's safety settings from the Family Safety website, accessible from any PC.

The Family Safety website not only enables parents to control everything their kids do on the internet, it also provides a degree of protection to the PC by blocking potentially dangerous downloads, and access to programs and settings on the PC.

Don't forget

A big advantage of the **Family Safety** website is that you can monitor and control your children's internet activities even when you are away from home by checking online at https://account. microsoft.com/family

Risk-Free Internet Browsing

The internet, as we all know, is the source of virtually all dangers faced by PC owners these days. No matter how tight your PC's security, no matter how careful you are, it is quite likely that something nasty will slip through the net.

So how is it possible to browse without any risk? The answer is to use a virtual PC when on the internet. To build one, you need a virtual machine application such as Oracle's **VirtualBox** – there are many others as well. These programs enable you to build a completely functional PC that runs within the program. Below, we see a virtual Windows 10 PC running in **VirtualBox** on a computer running another version of Windows:

If you are running Windows 10 Pro or Windows 10 Enterprise, you already have virtual machine software. You need to install it first though:

In the Taskbar **Search** box, type "Turn Windows features on or off". Click the link, check the **Hyper-V** box and click **OK**. When the feature has been installed, you'll see a new

Hyper-V Manager

Hyper-V Manager item under **Windows Administrative Tools** on the **Start** menu. This will enable the creation of a virtual computer.

By default, a virtual PC is completely isolated from the host PC (the physical machine), thus anything that happens on it, such as a virus, or malware, does not affect the host in any way. Furthermore, as you can install and run programs on a virtual PC, you can use it to evaluate downloaded software, safe in the knowledge that if the program is buggy, or otherwise suspect, it cannot mess up your physical computer. In fact, any action at all that you may be wary of trying on your main machine, such as changing system settings, messing in the Registry, etc., for fear of causing problems, can be tried out perfectly safely on a virtual machine first. If you are running Windows 10 Pro or Windows 10 Enterprise, you can use the **Hyper-V** virtual machine software built into Windows – see Hot tip. If not, use **VirtualBox** – a free download from **virtualbox.org**

9 Installation/ Setting Up

This chapter focuses on installation and setting up procedures. Among other things, you will learn the best way to install Windows 10, how to create a hard drive partition and calibrate a monitor.

Upgrading to Windows 10

When installing a new operating system, the option taken by most users is to simply install it over the top of the old one – a procedure known as upgrading.

The drawback with this method is that problems in the existing setup will be carried over to the new one. Typical examples of this are viruses and malware. There may also be third-party programs on the old setup that are corrupted and thus cause problems; these may also be carried over to the new setup. Furthermore, these issues can cause the installation of the new operating system to fail.

For these reasons, the best way of updating your operating system is to completely remove the old one first. Then, you install the new version. This method is known as a "clean install". However, there is a drawback – the procedure wipes the hard drive clean of all data, so you first have to make a backup of any data you don't want to lose and then reinstall all of your applications.

Because of this, you may prefer to go down the upgrade route instead, in which case we suggest you first carry out the following steps. This will greatly improve the chances of doing it successfully:

1 Optimize your hard drive by running a disk defragmentation utility, such as Windows **Disk Defragmenter**

2 Run a disk checking utility, such as Windows **Chkdsk** – hard drive errors are a common cause of installation problems

3 Check your system for viruses; these can stop an installation in its tracks. Having made sure your system is free of viruses, uninstall the antivirus program. Alternatively, you may be able to disable it in the BIOS. Antivirus software is well known for causing installation problems

4 Remove all programs from your Startup folder. Disconnect as much of your system's hardware as you can. Problems often occur during the hardware detection and configuration stages of an installation

Before carrying out a Windows reinstallation, make sure you back up your data. Although rare, an installation can result in data loss.

To run **Disk Defragmenter**, open **Computer/This PC** then right-click on the drive icon and choose **Properties** > **Tools** > **Optimize and defragment drive** > **Optimize**.

To run **CHKDSK**, open **Computer/This PC** then right-click on the drive icon and choose **Properties** > **Tools** > **Error checking** > **Check**.

Clean Installing Windows 10

There are two scenarios in which it may be necessary to do a clean installation of Windows. The first is when a new computer is being set up, and the second is when an existing installation is deleted and then replaced by a new copy because it is damaged.

With Windows 10, the latter is no longer necessary, as a feature called **Reset** reverts a Windows installation to original factory settings. In the first scenario, however, a clean installation is still necessary and this is how you do it:

 Start the PC and access the BIOS Setup program (see the first Hot tip). Open the Advanced BIOS Features page and scroll down to **First Boot Device**

```
            Phoenix - AwardBIOS CMOS Setup Utility

Virus Warning                [Disabled]
CPU Internal Cache           [Enabled]     Item Help
External Cache               [Enabled]
CPU L2 Cache ECC Checking    [Enabled]
Processor Number Feature     [Enabled]    Select Your Boot
Quick Power On Self Test     [Enabled]    Device Priority
First Boot Device            [CDROM]
Second Boot Device           [HDD-0]
Third Boot Device            [Floppy]
Boot Other Device            [Enabled]
Swap Floppy Drive            [Disabled]
Boot Up NumLock Status       [On]
Gate A20 Option              [Fast]
Ata 66/100 IDE Cable Msg.    [Enabled]
Typematic Rate Setting       [Disabled]
```

The BIOS access key is displayed on the first boot screen. It will also be in the motherboard manual – often it's the **Delete** key or **F1** key.

The BIOS screens on your PC may differ from the example on the left – it depends on the age of your PC and the BIOS manufacturer.

125

 Make sure **CDROM** is selected. If not, use the Page Up/ Page Down keys to select it. Save any changes made and exit the BIOS

Having set the CD/DVD drive as the first boot device, place the Windows 10 installation disk in the CD/DVD drive and boot the PC. Shortly afterwards, you will see a message saying "Press any key to boot from CD...". Do so, and Windows will begin loading its installation files to the hard drive.

 At the first screen, select your preferences – installation language, time and currency format, and keyboard method. At the next screen, click **Install now**

All the tools required to do a clean install of Windows 10 are on its installation disk. So, you must set the CD/DVD drive as the first boot device.

...cont'd

If your current operating system is Windows 7, you will see a "Drive 0 Partition 1: System Reserved" entry. This is not relevant to Windows 10 so you can either ignore it or you can delete it in the advanced drive options.

Don't forget

Your computer will reboot automatically during the installation procedure.

Hot tip

The end of the installation routine is signified by two screens – "Getting devices ready", followed by "Getting ready". The PC will then reboot into the new installation.

 Enter the product key to activate Windows and OK the license agreement, then in the next screen select **Custom: Install Windows only (advanced)**

Windows Setup

Which type of installation do you want?

Upgrade: Install Windows and keep files, settings, and applications
The files, settings, and applications are moved to Windows with this option. This option is only available when a supported version of Windows is already running on the computer.

Custom: Install Windows only (advanced)
The files, settings, and applications aren't moved to Windows with this option. If you want to make changes to partitions and drives, start the computer using the installation disc. We recommend backing up your files before you continue.

5 At the next screen, "Where do you want to install Windows?", select the required hard drive

Windows Setup

Where do you want to install Windows?

Name	Total size	Free space	Type
Drive 0 Partition 1: System Reserved	500.0 MB	235.0 MB	System
Drive 0 Partition 2	31.5 GB	24.8 GB	Primary

✦ Refresh   ✗ Delete   ✔ Format   ☀ New
🌐 Load driver   Extend

Next

 Click the **Format** link, then follow the prompts to complete the installation

Drive Management

The Windows **Drive Management** utility enables users to manage their hard drives. They can create, format and resize partitions, RAID (Redundant Array of Independent Disks) configurations, and create and manage Mounted and Dynamic partitions.

Much of this will be well above the average user's head and is, in any case, beyond the scope of this book to adequately address. Therefore, we will restrict ourselves to a brief explanation of how to access the utility, how to create and format new partitions, and resize existing partitions. These are the applications that the typical user will be interested in:

1 Go to **Control Panel** > **Administrative Tools**, then click **Computer Management**

2 When the **Computer Management** snap-in opens, click **Disk Management**

3 In the main window, you will see all the drives installed in the PC. The example below has an internal hard drive, an external hard drive, a USB drive, and a CD/DVD drive

You must have Administrator privileges to access the **Disk Management** utility.

You can also access the **Disk Management** utility by typing "diskmgmt.msc" into a Run box (**WinKey + R**).

To avoid any confusion, the term "Volume", as used in the right-click menu shown on the left, is Microsoft's parlance for a partition.

4 Right-click a drive to see the management options available to you

127

A partition is basically a container within a hard drive. Most PC manufacturers supply the PC with the hard drive partitioned to the maximum size, i.e. the full capacity of the drive. However, a partition can be split into any number of sub-partitions, each of which appears to Windows as a separate drive.

...cont'd

Creating a partition

In the example below, the PC has a single hard drive that has been partitioned to its maximum capacity. This means it has no free space. So before we can create another partition on the drive, we have to first create some free space to allocate to it. This will be taken from the unused space on the existing second partition.

1 Right-click the drive, then choose **Shrink Volume**

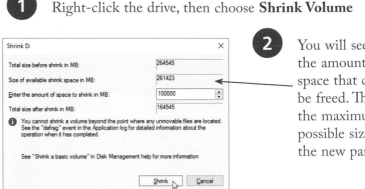

2 You will see the amount of space that can be freed. This is the maximum possible size of the new partition

3 Enter the amount of space you want to free up, then click the **Shrink** button. In the management window (below), you will now see the amount of space that has been freed

4 Right-click the area marked as **Unallocated** and select **New Simple Volume** – a wizard will now open

5 Click **Next** in each of the steps that follow, and then click **Finish**. The new partition will be created and formatted with the NTFS file system. In **This PC**, you will now see a new drive – this is the partition you've just created

Resizing a partition

To reduce the size of a partition, use the **Shrink Volume** command. To increase the size of one, first create some free space from a different partition, then right-click the partition and use the **Extend Volume** command to add the free space.

If you reduce the size of a partition, the amount by which it is reduced will become free space. Unless you use this free space to increase the size of a different partition or create a new one, it will be wasted.

Setting Up User Accounts

Windows allows the setting up of any number of user accounts, each of which can be individually configured in many ways (desktop icons, wallpapers, screensavers, and so on).

This feature is particularly useful in a home environment where several family members all use one PC. By giving each their own account, which they can customize to suit their specific requirements and tastes, a single PC can be used without conflict.

It can also be useful in a single-user environment by enabling a user to create accounts for specific purposes. For example, one account can be set up for photo-editing, with shortcuts to all the relevant programs placed on the Desktop. Another account can be set up as a home office, etc:

Hot tip

When two or more accounts are created, one of them must be an Administrator account. The person running this account will be able to set restrictions on what other account holders can and cannot do.

1 Go to **Settings** > **Accounts** > **Family & other people**, then under **Other people** click **Add someone else to this PC**

How will this person sign in?

Enter the email address or phone number of the person y
Windows, Office, Outlook.com, OneDrive, Skype, or Xbox,
number they use to sign in.

Email or phone

Let's create your account

Windows, Office, Outlook.com, OneDrive, Skype, Xbox. They're all better and more personal when you sign in with your Microsoft account.* Learn more

First name   Last name

someone@example.com

Get a new email address

Password

United States

Birth month   Day   Year

*If you already use a Microsoft service, go Back to sign in with that account.

Add a user without a Microsoft account

I don't have this person's sign-in information
Privacy statement

Next   Back

---

2 You will now have options of signing in with an existing Microsoft Account or creating a new one. You can also create a Local Account by opting to sign in without a Microsoft Account, plus create a child account

The disadvantage of a Local Account is that the user won't be able to download apps from the Windows Store, and also that they won't be able to synchronize their settings and data across different devices and computers.

Hot tip

A useful application of user accounts is to password-protect the main account, and then create standard accounts for the kids. They can use the PC but won't be able to compromise its security or performance, due to the limitations placed on standard accounts. (Also see pages 120-121.)

129

Create a Virtual Drive

Of critical importance in the increasingly digital world is how to keep digital data safe. Related factors include how and where to store the data and the cost of doing so.

We saw on page 33 how a technology known as RAID can be used to provide data protection. RAID is available in either software or hardware versions and, of the two, hardware is by far the most reliable, as it is completely independent of the operating system. The problem with hardware RAID is that it requires a separate RAID controller card and good ones are not cheap.

A feature in Windows 10 provides a much more cost-effective method of data protection, although, being a software solution, it is still not as robust as hardware RAID. The feature is known as **Storage Spaces** and can be accessed in the **Control Panel**.

Storage Spaces provides three very useful benefits – an easily-expandable space in which to store data, RAID data protection, and low cost.

Expandable Space

A Storage Space is essentially a virtual drive comprised of a number of physical drives. The drives can be of any type, e.g. SATA, USB, SAS, etc., and of any size. The capacities of the drives are combined to produce a Storage Space. The capacity of the Storage Space can be increased at any time by simply adding another drive – this is its main advantage; a single drive of unlimited capacity can be created quickly and easily.

The capacity of a Storage Space is set by the user, and it is not restricted to the total capacity of the physical drives. For example, a 100GB Storage Space can be created from 10GB of physical drive space. This is achieved with a technique known as "thin provisioning", which gives the appearance of more space than actually exists. As more data is added to the Storage Space, or virtual disk, the size of the real file grows as necessary.

When the capacity of a Storage Space has been used up, it can be reset to a larger size.

Data Protection

When a Storage Space is created, the user has the option to add data protection of the same type used in RAID.

The advantage of an expandable space is simplified storage management.

One caveat with **Storage Spaces** is that they are not bootable, i.e. you cannot install an operating system on one.

You can mix and match drives of any type and size when creating **Storage Spaces**.

Three types of fault tolerance are offered: **Simple** (striping), **Mirror** and **Parity** (see Hot tips). For example, with 2-way mirroring, two copies of a space's data are stored on separate drives. Thus, if one drive fails, the data is recoverable from the other.

Cost

Storage Spaces offers nothing that cannot be found elsewhere – there are quite a few other companies offering similar products. However, without exception, these cost hundreds of dollars, require specific hardware, and provide expansion options that are limited in scope.

Storage Spaces, on the other hand, costs nothing, requires no hardware other than the drives, provides a virtual drive of unlimited size, and is very simple and quick to set up. The procedure is:

1 Go to **Control Panel** > **Storage Spaces**, then choose **Create a new pool and storage space** – to see the drives on your system that are compatible with **Storage Spaces**:

📇 Create a storage pool	— □ ×

← → ∨ ↑ 📇 « Storage Spaces › Create a storage pool   ∨ ↻   Search Control Panel   🔎

Select drives to create a storage pool

Formatted drives   ⌃

⚠ The following drives might contain files. If you use a formatted drive with a storage pool, Windows permanently deletes all the files on that drive. You can't recover the files by using the Recycle Bin.

☑ 🖴   Toshiba 2.5"External Har ...   Disk 2   View files
           Attached via USB   Online   Take offline
           465 GB

                                        Create pool   Cancel

2 Select the drives you want to use for the Storage Space and click **Create pool**

3 In the new window, you will see options for the drive letter to use, the type of resiliency (simple, two-way mirror, etc.), and the size of the pool. When you have made your choices, click **Create Storage Space**

Transfer everything to easily keep your user accounts, Settings, Documents, Music, Email, Pictures, and Video.

The **Windows Easy Transfer** utility, found in earlier versions of Windows, is not available in Windows 10.

Choose to transfer via Wi-Fi or Ethernet cable. Another good way is to use a Laplink USB cable (this has a USB plug on either end).

Keep Your Files & Settings

One of these days you're going to decide that you need a new computer. Having bought it, you will then need to redo all of the customization and configuration settings, such as internet/email settings, display settings, Taskbar configuration, and so on. You will also have to transfer all of your files, such as music and video, to the new PC. It will be a time-consuming process.

The **OneDrive** app in Windows 10 will help enormously. By default, all of your personalization and app settings, plus other stuff such as internet favorites and history, passwords, and many other Windows settings are automatically saved to your **OneDrive** storage account. All you have to do is configure the new PC with the same Microsoft Account used on the old PC, and all the settings will be seamlessly transferred to it.

With regard to transferring your data, this is easy with the **PCmover Express** utility. The Personal Use edition is available free from **http://pcmover10.laplink.com**, and works like this:

1 Install **PCmover Express** on both your old and new computers

2 Run the utility and select the transfer connection type

3 Follow the wizard steps, and your new computer will have the same personality and functionality as your old PC

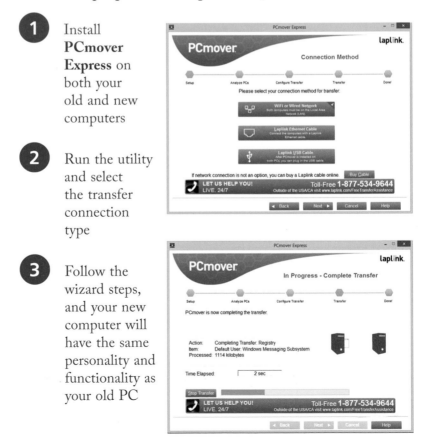

Run Older Programs on Windows 10

When you install programs on your Windows 10 PC, you may come across one or two that refuse to run – this will be due to incompatibility issues. Before you give up on them, try installing them with the Compatibility Mode wizard. This will recreate the Windows environment for which they were designed and will, in most cases, get them running.

1 Go to **Control Panel** > **Security and Maintenance**. At the bottom-left, click **Windows Program Compatibility Troubleshooter**, then click **Next**

2 After a few moments you will see a dialog box showing you a list of all the programs on the PC. Select the one you're having trouble with, and then click **Next**

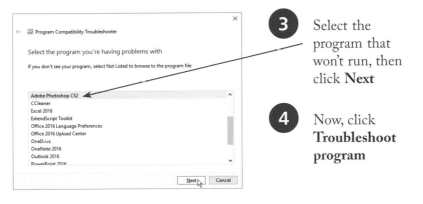

3 Select the program that won't run, then click **Next**

4 Now, click **Troubleshoot program**

5 Check the appropriate problem from the list, then click **Next** to have Windows attempt to fix the issue

Don't forget

Once a program has been set up successfully, it will use the compatibility settings every time it is run.

Beware

If a program won't install at all, the method described here won't work. In this case, do it as described in the Hot tip below.

Hot tip

Another way of applying compatibility settings is to right-click the program's executable (setup) file. Click **Properties** and then open the **Compatibility** tab. From here, you can choose an operating system that the program is known to work with.

6 To retry, click **Yes, try again using different settings**

Install Windows 10 Quickly

Here, we show you how to install Windows 10 from a USB flash drive. The advantages of installing Windows in this way are threefold:

● Speed – Windows will install much quicker

● You will have a much more robust copy of the installation disk (which you can now put in a drawer and forget about)

● You can install Windows on PCs with no DVD drive

Microsoft provides the **Windows 10 Media Creation Tool** that enables you to easily create bootable USB installation media:

Before installing Windows 10 you should ensure the PC meets the system requirements for Windows 10 – see microsoft.com/en-us/ windows/windows-10-specifications

1 Open your web browser and navigate to **microsoft.com/en-us/software-download/windows10**

2 Next, click the button labeled **Download tool now**

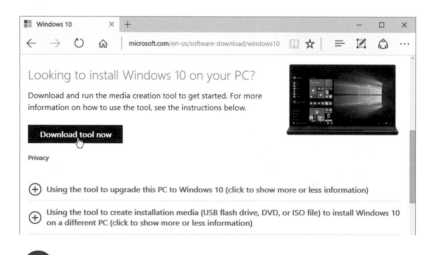

Installation requires a product key. If you don't already have one you can select **I need to buy a product key** during the installation procedure.

3 When the download completes, select **Run** then click **Accept** to agree the license terms

4 On the "What do you want to do?" page, select **Create installation media for another PC**, then click **Next**

5 Now, choose the language, architecture, and edition you require (for example **English (US)**, **Windows 10**, **x64**), then click **Next** to continue

6 On the "Choose which media to use" page, select the
USB flash drive option

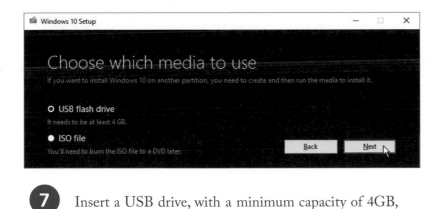

The USB drive must have
a capacity of no less
than 4GB and should be
blank – any existing data
already on the drive will
be lost in this process.

7 Insert a USB drive, with a minimum capacity of 4GB,
then click **Next**

8 Confirm the correct drive in the "Removable drives" list,
then click **Next** to download Windows 10

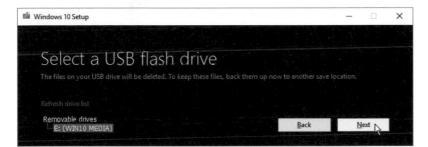

9 When the download has completed, attach the USB drive
to the PC where you want to install Windows 10

10 Restart the PC, then press any key to boot from the USB
installation media

If the current version of
Windows starts when
you restart the PC you
may have to change the
boot order in the BIOS
to make the USB drive
the First Boot Device –
see page 125.

11 On the "Install Windows" page, select your language,
time, and keyboard preferences, then click **Next**

12 Choose **Install Windows** and complete the wizard steps

Calibrate Your Monitor

Have you ever noticed when printing an image that the print-out looks somewhat different to the image on the PC? For example: it's brighter or darker, the colors aren't the same, or it looks washed-out?

It could be that the printer settings are not correct, but it's far more likely that your monitor is incorrectly calibrated. Windows 10 includes a Monitor Calibration utility, and you can access it by going to **Control Panel** > **Display**. At the top-left of the **Display** dialog box, click **Calibrate color**. You will then be taken through a series of dialog boxes:

Hot tip

Before calibrating your monitor, allow the monitor to warm up for at least 30 minutes so that it's at its full operating temperature. This will ensure a consistent display.

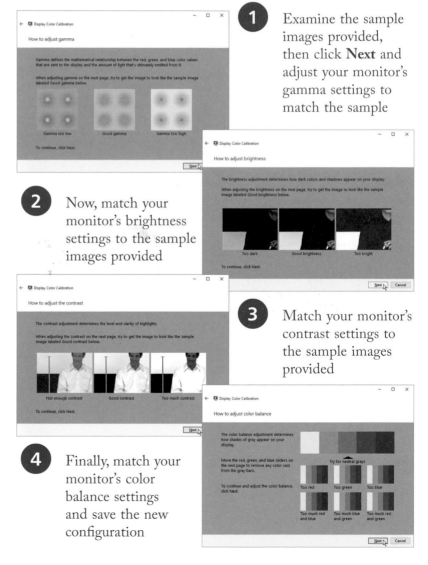

1 Examine the sample images provided, then click **Next** and adjust your monitor's gamma settings to match the sample

2 Now, match your monitor's brightness settings to the sample images provided

3 Match your monitor's contrast settings to the sample images provided

4 Finally, match your monitor's color balance settings and save the new configuration

Hot tip

When calibrating your monitor, set your desktop background to a neutral gray. Bright colors and patterns surrounding an image make it difficult to accurately perceive color.

10 Shortcuts

Virtually every action that can be done with a mouse can also be done with a keyboard. This chapter shows how, and also explains some other useful shortcuts.

Switch Applications Quickly

Virtual desktops have been available in other operating systems for quite some time but are new in Windows 10.

Hot tip

You can also access **Task View** by pressing **WinKey + Tab**, and you can move between desktops by holding down **Ctrl + WinKey** then pressing the left or right arrow keys.

Windows 10 has a virtual desktop feature called "Task View". This allows you to have multiple desktops so you can spread out various projects, so that each project is on a separate desktop. When you need to jump from one project to another you can just switch desktops and everything is right there waiting for you – no need to minimize and maximize windows to get back to work:

1 Click the ▭ button on the Taskbar to access the **Task View** feature – thumbnails of all running apps and a **+ New desktop** button appear on the screen

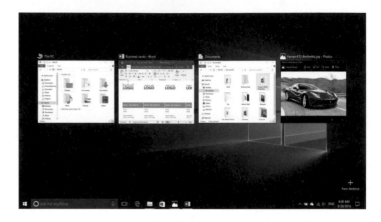

2 Next, click the **+ New Desktop** button – thumbnails of the original desktop and a new, blank desktop appear in a bar across the bottom of the screen

3 Each desktop thumbnail has a pop-up **X** button which you can use to close that desktop

Hot tip

The old Flip feature is still available too – hold down **Alt** then hit **Tab** to switch between desktop thumbnails of your running apps.

4 Select any desktop thumbnail to switch to that desktop, where you can open apps and move apps from one desktop to another

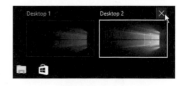

One-Click Shutdown/Restart

Users who like to do things quickly will appreciate the following method of instantly shutting down, restarting or logging off.

Shutdown

1 Create a desktop shortcut (right-click, **New > Shortcut**) and type **SHUTDOWN -s -t 01** into the box:

> ← **Create Shortcut**   ×
>
> **What item would you like to create a shortcut for?**
> This wizard helps you to create shortcuts to local or network programs, files, folders, computers, or Internet addresses.
>
> Type the location of the item:
>
> `SHUTDOWN -s -t 01`   [Browse...]

2 Click **Next**, name the shortcut "Shut Down", then click **Finish**

Restart

As above but this time type **SHUTDOWN -r -t 01** in the box. Name this shortcut "Restart".

Log Off

As above, but this time type **LOGOFF** in the box. Name it "Log Off".

When you have finished, you will see these icons on the Desktop:

Log Off   Restart   Shut Down

Using the steps detailed on page 92, you can change the icons to something more interesting or representative, as shown below:

Log Off   Restart   Shut Down

Beware

Be sure to type these commands precisely, including spaces, or they will not work.

Hot tip

You can also create hotkey shortcuts for your **Shut Down**, **Restart** and **Log Off** commands – see page 140.

Hot tip

Drag the icons to the Taskbar to make them more readily accessible.

Hotkey Shortcuts

There will be occasions when you want to open a program, but don't wish to close the current window to get to it. For example, you may be doing a tax return online and need to open the calculator.

A hotkey shortcut is the answer:

 Right-click the Desktop and choose **New > Shortcut**, then type "calc.exe" in the location box

 Click **Next** and name the shortcut "Calculator", then click the **Finish** button

 Now, right-click the shortcut icon and select **Properties** – to open its **Properties** dialog box

 Click in the **Shortcut key** box (this will be reading **None**)

Hot tip

You can use the steps on this page to open your favorite websites with a combination keystroke. Create a shortcut with a web page URL in the location box. Right-click the shortcut, choose **Properties** and click the **Web Document** tab. Then, follow Steps 4-7 to assign a shortcut key to the web page.

Hot tip

If your keyboard came with a software disk, you may find that it contains a program that enables you to create hotkey shortcuts with the F keys.

5 Now, do not type into the box, but simply press the key you want to use as the shortcut key – we pressed the "C" key in the example here

6 The **Shortcut key** box will now read **Ctrl + Alt + C**

Calculator Properties ×

General | Shortcut | Security | Details | Previous Versions

Calculator

Target type: Application

Target location: System32

Target: C:\Windows\System32\calc.exe

Start in: C:\Windows\system32

Shortcut key: Ctrl + Alt + C

Run: Normal window

Comment:

Open File Location | Change Icon... | Advanced...

OK | Cancel | Apply

7 Click **Apply** then click **OK**. From now on, you can open the application by pressing **Ctrl + Alt + C**

Windows Key Shortcuts

Most standard keyboards have one, or even two, Windows keys. These are situated near the space bar and have a logo of a flying window printed on them. The key is commonly known as the "WinKey".

Windows keys

With either of these keys you can quickly open a number of applications on your computer.

The table below shows which keys can be used in conjunction with the Windows key and what they do:

Keys	Action
WinKey + Tab	Open/close Task View
WinKey + A	Open/close Action Center
WinKey + C	Open Cortana, with speech
WinKey + D	Minimize/restore all windows
WinKey + E	Open File Explorer
WinKey + G	Open/close the Xbox game bar
WinKey + I	Open Windows Settings
WinKey + L	Lock the computer
WinKey + P	Open Project screen options
WinKey + R	Open the Run dialog box
WinKey + S	Open Search
WinKey + T	Cycle through Taskbar programs
WinKey + U	Open Ease of Access Center
WinKey + X	Open the Power User Menu

Hot tip

On its own, press the **WinKey** at any time to open the Start menu.

Hot tip

Keyboard shortcuts can also be found within applications. Alongside most menu commands, you will see shortcut key combinations.

NEW

The Xbox game bar (**WinKey + G**) is a new feature in Windows 10 that allows you to record game action and take screenshots of games.

Easy Email

This is a handy tip for those of you who do a lot of emailing. Instead of starting your email program each time you want to send a message to someone and then clicking the Create Mail button on the menu bar, you can achieve the same result from the Desktop with one double-click. Here's how to do it:

1 Right-click the Desktop and select **New > Shortcut**. You will see the following dialog box

2 In the location box, type "mailto:", then click **Next**

3 Now, give the shortcut a suitable name, such as "Write Email"

4 You will now see a new email icon on the Desktop. Double-click it, and an open email message window will appear

Taking this a step further, you can have the message window open with the address already filled in. Do this by entering the email address immediately after "mailto:". For example, if you enter "mailto:info@ineasysteps.com" your email will open with this address in the **To:** box, as shown below – type in your message and click **Send**.

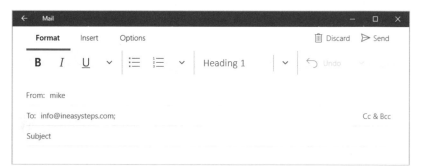

Taskbar Searching

A rarely used feature in Windows 10 is the **Address** toolbar. This lets you do a number of things directly from the Desktop:

 Right-click the Taskbar and select **Toolbars** > **Address**. You will now see an Address box on the Taskbar next to the notification area

The first thing you can use the **Address** toolbar for is to launch websites – you don't need to open your web browser first. Just type in the address and hit **Enter**, or click the arrow.

Furthermore, once you've launched a site in this way, you can subsequently relaunch it by clicking the down arrow at the side of the box and selecting the site from the history list.

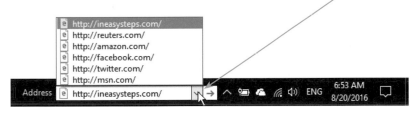

You can also conduct an internet search from the **Address** toolbar. To do this, just enter your search keyword and hit **Enter** on the keyboard:

Microsoft's default search engine, **Bing**, will open with the results of the search.

Finally, you can launch programs from the **Address** toolbar if you know their executable name. For example, type "winword" and hit **Enter** to open Microsoft Word.

There's nothing you can do with the **Address** toolbar that you can't do elsewhere, but it has the advantage of being more readily accessible.

You can click the → "Go to" arrow at the right of the **Address** bar instead of hitting the **Enter** key.

The **Address** toolbar can be used like the Run box – for example, you can enter "regedit" in the **Address** bar to open the Registry Editor.

Keyboard Shortcuts

In certain situations, using the keyboard can be a much easier way of controlling a computer. The following is a selection of useful keyboard shortcuts:

Hot tip

Below are some useful shortcuts that work with most applications:

• **Ctrl + O** – opens a document from within a program

• **Ctrl + N** – opens a new document

• **Ctrl + S** – saves work in progress

144

Don't forget

The **Alt + Tab** shortcut doesn't need both keys pressed at once – hold down the **Alt** key then tap the **Tab** key to switch between thumbnails.

General Shortcuts	
Ctrl + C	Copy the selected item
Ctrl + X	Cut the selected item
Ctrl + V	Paste the selected item
Ctrl + Z	Undo the last action
Delete	Delete the selected item
Shift + Delete	Delete an item permanently
F2	Rename the selected item
Ctrl + right arrow	Move to the beginning of the next word
Ctrl + left arrow	Move to the beginning of the previous word
Ctrl + down arrow	Move to the beginning of the next paragraph
Ctrl + up arrow	Move to the beginning of the previous paragraph
Ctrl + Shift + arrow	Select a block of text
Ctrl + A	Select all items in a document or window
F3	Search for a file or folder
Alt + Enter	Display properties for the selected item
Alt + F4	Close the active item or exit the active program
Alt + spacebar	Open the shortcut menu for the active window
Ctrl + F4	Close the active document
Alt + Tab	Switch between open items
Ctrl + Alt + Tab	Use the arrow keys to switch between open items
Alt + Esc	Cycle through items in the order they were opened
F6	Cycle through screen elements in a window
F4	Display the Address bar list in File Explorer
Shift + F10	Display the shortcut menu for the selected item
Ctrl + Esc	Open the Start menu
F10	Activate the menu bar in the active program
Right arrow	Open the menu to the right, or open a sub-menu
Left arrow	Open the menu to the left, or close a sub-menu
F5	Refresh the active window
Alt + up arrow	View the folder one level up in File Explorer
ESC	Cancel the current task
Ctrl + Shift + Esc	Open the Task Manager
Shift (when inserting a CD)	Prevent the CD from automatically playing

Microsoft Edge Shortcuts	
Tab	Move forward through items
Shift + Tab	Move backwards through items
Alt + Home	Go to your home page
Alt + right arrow	Go to the next page opened in the tab
Backspace	Go to the previous page opened in the tab
Up arrow	Move toward the beginning of a web page
Down arrow	Move toward the end of a web page
Home	Move to the beginning of a web page
End	Move to the end of a web page
Enter	Activate a selected link
F5	Refresh the current web page
F12	Open/Close Developer Tools
Esc	Stop downloading a page
Ctrl + D	Add site to Favorites
Ctrl + E	Open search from Address bar
Ctrl + F	Find on this page
Ctrl + H	Open History
Ctrl + I	Open Favorites
Ctrl + J	Open Downloads
Ctrl + K	Duplicate current tab
Ctrl + N	Open new window
Ctrl + P	Open Print dialog
Ctrl + R	Restore current page
Ctrl + click	Open links in a new tab in the background
Ctrl + Shift + click	Open links in a new tab in the foreground
Ctrl + T	Open a new tab in the foreground
Ctrl + Tab	Switch between tabs
Ctrl + W	Close current tab
Alt + Enter	Open a new tab in the foreground from the Address bar
Ctrl + 9	Switch to the last tab
Ctrl + F4	Close active tab
Alt + D	Select the text in the Address bar
F4	Display a list of addresses you've typed
Ctrl + Enter	Add "www." and ".com"

Don't forget

Many Microsoft Edge operations are actually quicker using the keyboard. For example, the **Backspace** key is much easier to use than the **Back** button. Also, try using the **Up** and **Down** arrow keys to scroll through pages. The **Home** and **End** keys are other useful keys that take you quickly to the beginning and end of pages.

Hot tip

The list on this page contains just some of the keyboard shortcuts available for Microsoft Edge and Internet Explorer. You can find many more by going to **windows.microsoft. com/en-us/windows/ keyboard-shortcuts**

...cont'd

New Windows 10 Interface Shortcuts	
WinKey	Open/close the Start menu
WinKey + A	Open the Action Center
WinKey + C	Open Cortana, with speech recognition
WinKey + D	Show the Desktop
WinKey + E	Open File Explorer
WinKey + G	Open the Xbox game bar
WinKey + H	Open the Share feature, to share content
WinKey + I	Open Windows Settings
WinKey + K	Open the Connect feature, to stream media
WinKey + L	Lock the computer
WinKey + M	Minimize the current window
WinKey + N	Open OneNote
WinKey + P	Open the Project feature, to switch displays
WinKey + Q	Open the Search panel
WinKey + R	Open the Run box
WinKey + S	Open Cortana, without speech recognition
WinKey + T	Cycle through Taskbar icons
WinKey + U	Open the Ease of Access Center
WinKey + X	Open the Power User Menu
WinKey + Ctrl + D	Create a new virtual desktop
WinKey + Ctrl + F4	Close the current virtual desktop
WinKey + Ctrl + left/right	Move between virtual desktops
WinKey + Shift + left/right	Move apps between monitors
WinKey + arrow key	Snap window to left/right/top/bottom
WinKey + number key	Open apps on the Taskbar, first is number 1
WinKey + spacebar	Switch input language and keyboard layout
WinKey + Tab	Open Task View

The most useful of these keyboard shortcuts is the **WinKey** by itself, which opens the Start menu, and the ones that open the various Windows menus, such as **WinKey + C** (Cortana with speech), **WinKey + R** (Run box) and **WinKey + E** (File Explorer).

Hot tip

Type the main part of an address and then press **Ctrl + Enter**. This will automatically add the www. and .com to complete the address. This only works for addresses ending with **.com**, however.

146

Don't forget

Press **WinKey + Tab** to open **Task View**, then use the arrow keys to switch between thumbnails, and press **Enter** to select the current thumbnail app.

11 The Internet

The internet is a wonderful resource for information, entertainment, software and business. This chapter details a wide range of tips that include extending the basic functionality of Microsoft Edge, useful features of this new browser, and how to improve the efficiency with which you use the internet.

No More Broken Downloads

Anyone who downloads data from the internet will, at one time or another, experience the irritation of an unexpected disruption to their download.

Unfortunately, Microsoft Edge doesn't have the ability to automatically resume interrupted downloads, so you then have initiate the process again. Furthermore, it may be necessary to start the download from the beginning. This is not too bad if it is a small download, but if you are downloading a large file, you could have wasted a lot of time.

The solution is to use what's known as a "download manager". Programs of this type monitor a download, and if it is interrupted for whatever reason, will resume it from the point at which the download stopped – thus, you don't have to start again from the beginning.

They also offer other useful features, such as automatic scheduling, automatic redial (for dial-up modem connections) and details regarding file size, download time, and so on.

One of the most popular download programs is the **GetRight** download manager (shown below), available at **getright.com**

Download managers can be configured to begin a download at a specified time. They will automatically initiate the internet connection, begin the download, and when it is completed, end the connection. If your connection should fail during the download, they will attempt to reconnect and then resume the download.

A handy feature offered by most download managers is the drop-target. This is a small icon that can be placed anywhere on the screen. Download links are simply dragged to it and then released.

A good download manager can also increase download speeds considerably. If the file is held on several servers (which is quite common), the program will switch between the servers, automatically selecting the one that offers the best, i.e. fastest, download conditions.

Cut Down on the Scrolling

Have you ever opened one of those web pages that seems to go on forever? To find something specific, you have to keep scrolling down the page and, if you miss it, then scroll back up.

Let's say you are researching an article on the Confederate States of America. Your search leads you to one of these long pages, the content of which is the American Civil War. All you want is information about the Confederate States, and nothing else. So, instead of endless scrolling down the page to find references to them, try the following:

 On the keyboard, press **Ctrl + F**

Just below the address box, you will now see a **Find** toolbar.

2 Type "Confederate" into the Search box

Microsoft Edge will automatically highlight all text instances of the word or phrase entered in yellow – so you can't miss them. Additionally, it displays a count of the total number of instances found alongside the Search box on the **Find** toolbar.

3 To go to the next instance found, press the > forward arrow button that appears after the counter display

4 Press the > forward button to move to the next instance, or press the < back button to return to the previous one

The **Find** toolbar provides a drop-down menu to **Match whole word** and/or **Match case** to refine your search within the page.

You can also open the **Find** toolbar in Microsoft Edge by pressing the **F3** function key.

The **Find** feature will automatically scroll the page up and down as you click the arrow buttons to reveal the next instance found.

You can also navigate the search results using keyboard shortcuts. Hit Enter to move forward or Shift + Enter to move back, and hit Esc to exit the search.

Disable SmartScreen

SmartScreen is a feature that provides the Microsoft Edge web browser with these three main functions:

● As the user browses the internet, it analyzes the web pages for signs of anything suspicious

● It checks all sites visited against a dynamic and continuously updated list of known phishing sites

● It checks all files downloaded from the internet against a list of known malicious malware

Windows 10, however, takes **SmartScreen** a step further by integrating it into the operating system itself. As a result, in addition to the above, it will automatically block attempts to run any program that it doesn't recognize.

While the blocking can be overridden, many users are going to find the need to do so irritating and unnecessary. For those who don't need it, **SmartScreen** can be disabled:

1 Go to **Control Panel** > **Security and Maintenance**

2 Click the **Change Windows SmartScreen settings** link

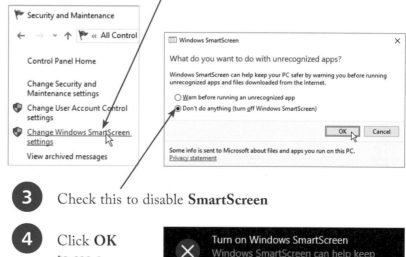

3 Check this to disable **SmartScreen**

4 Click **OK** to see a notification reminder

Beware

Phishing is a scam that works by setting up a fake website identical to that of a respected institution, such as a bank. Victims are sent an email with a link to the fake website asking them to log on. When they do, their username and password are stolen. The consequences of this are obvious.

Beware

Users for whom privacy is an issue should be aware that **SmartScreen** automatically sends data to Microsoft about every application the user installs.

Keep Up with the News

Many websites, such as news agencies, offer a service called **RSS Feeds**. This service automatically feeds information, such as news headlines, sports scores, etc. at regular intervals to interested subscribers. The Microsoft Edge web browser does not currently support **RSS Feeds** but Internet Explorer has a built-in RSS reader that enables users to subscribe to, and read, any number of RSS Feeds without having to visit the websites providing them.

To use this feature, you first have to find an **RSS Feeds** service and then subscribe to it:

1 When you visit a website that provides a feed, the **RSS Feed** button will turn orange. Click the button to see what the feed offers, then click the feed itself

2 A new window will open showing all the articles available in the feed. Click the **Subscribe to this feed** link

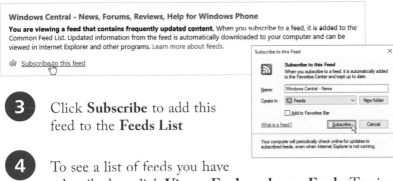

3 Click **Subscribe** to add this feed to the **Feeds List**

4 To see a list of feeds you have subscribed to click **View** > **Explorer bars** > **Feeds**. To view one, click it and Internet Explorer will open the page

An add-on extension may be released later to support **RSS Feeds** in Microsoft Edge.

Feeds work best with a broadband connection.

You can also configure Internet Explorer to play an alerting sound when you open a web page that contains a feed. Go to **Internet Options** in the Control Panel and click the **Content** tab. Then, click **Settings** under Feeds.

File Sharing

File sharing is a very popular internet activity. It makes use of specialized peer-to-peer networks and software, which allow users to connect directly to the computers of other users in the same network. The purpose of it all lies in the name – file sharing. Each user can designate specific files on their PC which they are willing to share.

To take part in this activity, you need a file sharing program. These are available as a free download on the internet and there are dozens of them (go to **download.com** and enter "file sharing" in the Search box).

Simply download and install the program, designate which files you want to share with other users, and you're all set to go. Good examples of this type of application are **BitLord** (**bitlord.com**) and **Emule** (**emule-project.net**).

Of all the file sharing programs, **Emule** (shown below) is considered to be the best. It is also free of all adware and spyware; something that cannot be said for many of them.

To get the best out of file sharing, you really need a broadband connection, as many of the files available for download can be several gigabytes in size.

File sharing networks are awash with viruses and malware. Not only that, but the file sharing programs themselves may add malware to your system. Don't get involved in this activity if you want to keep your PC as clean as possible.

Unauthorized copying or distribution of copyrighted material is illegal. Ensure you only share files legally.

When using these programs, there are two things to be aware of:

- **Malware** – some file sharing programs may attempt to install malware onto your PC... be wary of this!

- **Copyright** – while the use of the program is legal, the downloading of copyrighted material is not... do this at your own risk!

Get More Search Providers

A useful feature in Microsoft Edge is the ability to search directly from the Address bar – there's no need to go to a search engine. Not surprisingly, though, results from a search are taken from Microsoft's search engine, **Bing**. Should you wish to use a different search engine, you can set this up as described below:

1 Open Microsoft Edge and browse to the search engine you wish to add. For example, visit **google.com**

2 At the top-right of the Microsoft Edge window, click the **...** (**More options**) button, then choose the **Settings** option

3 Under "Advanced settings" click **View advanced settings**

4 Under "Search in the address bar with", click the **Change search engine** button

5 Select the search engine you want to add, then click the **Set as default** button

6 Perform a search in the Address bar, to now see the results are returned by your chosen search engine

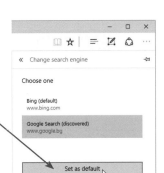

Hot tip

Additional search engines get appended to the **Search in the address bar with** list – so you can easily switch back to Bing, or any other search engine within that list.

153

Hot tip

If outside the USA, entering the address **google.com** may redirect you to the local Google page of your country. If you do not want to do this, enter **google.com/ncr** (no country redirect) instead.

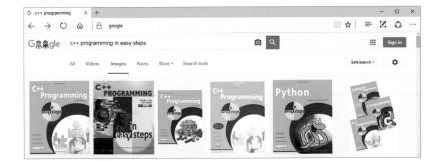

Quick Internet Searching

Type the word "tiger" into **Bing** or **Google** and you will get millions of pages to look through. These will range from the Tiger Stores in Spain, to Tigerair in Singapore, to pages about tiger animals. Finding something specific may take a long time.

To help users narrow their searches, all of the major search engines offer an Advanced Search. This will offer various options, such as language-specific searches, and searches restricted to pages updated within a specific time frame, etc.

Different search engines work in different ways. For example, with some, the + operator is used by default, while with others, it isn't.

Top 5 search engines:
Google.com
Bing.com
Yahoo.com
Ask.com
Duckduckgo.com

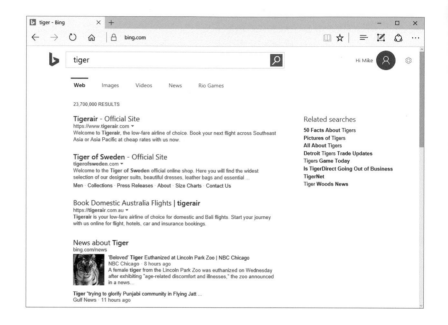

However, before you try these, the following simple search aids may be all you need.

The + Operator

Most search engines exclude common words such as "and" and "to", and certain single digits and letters. If you want to make sure a common word is included in the search, type + before it.

For example:

world war +1

(make sure there is a space between the + and the previous word).

A "Search Site" feature found in the Google Toolbar (**toolbar.google. com**) enables a user to search within a specific website, even if the website does not provide a search engine of its own.

...cont'd

The - Operator

The - operator allows you to exclude words from a search. For example, if you are looking for windows (glass ones), type:

windows -microsoft

This will eliminate millions of pages devoted to the various Windows operating systems.

The Or Operator

The **or** operator allows you to search for pages that contain word A **or** word B **or** word C, etc. For example, to search for camping trips in either Yosemite or Yellowstone national parks, you would type the following:

"camping trips" yosemite or yellowstone

Phrase Searches

By enclosing your keywords in quotation marks, you can do a phrase search. This will return pages with all the keywords in the order entered.

For example, **"atlanta falcons"** will return pages mainly concerning the Atlanta NFL team. Most pages regarding Atlanta (the city) or Falcons (the birds) will be excluded.

Combinations of Operators

To further narrow your searches, you can use combinations of search operators and phrase searches. Using our atlanta falcons example, you can remove several million search results by typing:

"atlanta falcons" -olympic games -birds of prey -city

Numeric Range Searches

Numeric range searches can be used to ensure that search results contain numbers within a specified range. You can conduct a numeric range search by specifying two numbers, separated by two periods with no spaces.

For example, you would search for computers in the $600 to $900 price bracket by typing **computers $600..900**

Numeric range can be used for all types of units (monetary, weight, measurement, and so on).

You may, at some stage, come across the phrase "Boolean Operators" with regard to search engines. These are derived from Boolean Logic, which is a system for establishing relationships between terms. The three main Boolean operators are:

- Or
- And (equivalent to +)
- Not (equivalent to -)

The most useful operators are: - (Not), and quotation marks (phrase searching). These two operators can whittle search results that would otherwise be several million, down to a few hundred pages.

155

Easy Text Selection

When selecting text in a web page it can be difficult to select precisely what you want, without also selecting adjacent text, and objects such as images and tables, as shown below:

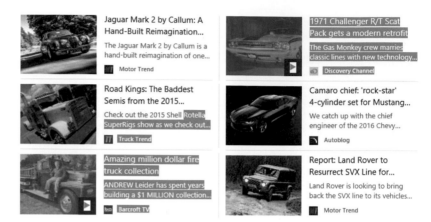

You will not be able to select text that appears within an image. You can only select actual text content in a web page.

With Microsoft Edge, the Caret Browsing feature helps solve this problem. This lets you use the keyboard instead of the mouse to make selections and it offers much more precise control:

1   Place the cursor at the beginning of the text block you want to select

2   Press **F7** to open the **Turn on caret browsing?** dialog box

Hold down the **Shift** key and select characters with the **Forward/Back** keys or select lines with the **Up/Down** keys.

3   Check **Don't ask me again when I press F7** if you want to use Caret Browsing often

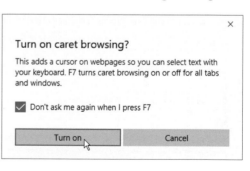

Turn on caret browsing?

This adds a cursor on webpages so you can select text with your keyboard. F7 turns caret browsing on or off for all tabs and windows.

☑ Don't ask me again when I press F7

[Turn on]   [Cancel]

4   Next, click the **Turn on** button to activate Caret Browsing

Once Caret Browsing has been turned on you can press F7 at any time to turn it off and on.

5   Hold down the Shift key and highlight the text with the arrow keys

Get to Grips with Tabs

Browser tabs are another useful feature in Microsoft Edge. Using them is straightforward enough, so rather than describing the obvious, we'll show you a neat trick you may not have noticed yet.

Rather than having Microsoft Edge open with one default page, tabs allow you to have as many as you want:

1 Click **...** (**More options**) > **Settings**, then under "Open Microsoft Edge with" select **A specific page or pages**

2 Click the input box that now appears, inviting you to "Enter a URL"

3 Type the URL address of a website to open in a tab, then click the + **Add new page** button – to see another new input box appear below your entry

4 Repeat Step 3 for as many tabs as you would like to add

The next time you start Microsoft Edge, it will automatically open all websites on the list, each in a separate tabbed window.

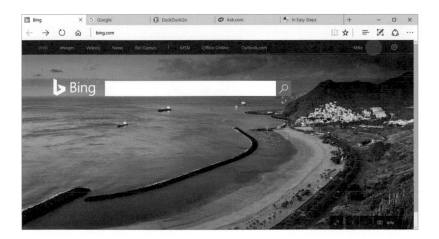

157

Hot tip

To close a specific tab when you have several open, you have to click the tab in order to reveal the X button. A quicker way is to click anywhere in the tab with the mouse's scroll wheel.

Hot tip

Notice that the tabs are arranged in the same order as they are listed in Settings. Make your preferred tab the first list item to see it open on top every time you start Microsoft Edge.

Reading List is a new feature in Microsoft Edge on Windows 10.

Don't confuse the **Reading List** (for saved articles) with the **Reading View** – for easy page viewing (see next page).

Remove a saved article from the **Reading List** by right-clicking on it and choosing **Delete** from the context menu.

Reading Articles

When you discover an article of interest that you don't have time to read right away, you can save it to your **Reading List** for later:

 Open the website, then click the star button on the  Edge web browser's toolbar – to open a Hub pane

 On the Hub pane, click the **Reading List** button

3 Edit the article **Name**, then click the **Add** button

4 To open a saved article, first click the **Hub** button

5 Next, click the **Reading List** icon to see saved articles

6 Now, click the saved article from the displayed list to open that website once more

...cont'd

Microsoft Edge provides a **Reading View** option that lets you read articles in a distraction-free format that you can customize:

1 Open the website, then click the **Reading View** icon to switch to the default textual content display mode

Reading View is a new feature in Microsoft Edge on Windows 10.

2 Click the **...** (**More options**) button, then choose **Settings**

3 Scroll down to the **Reading** section, then adjust the **Reading view style** to suit your preference for how the page content is displayed

You can also use the keyboard shortcut **Ctrl + Shift + R** to see the **Reading View**.

159

Your chosen **Reading** settings will be used for **Reading View** each time you choose that option.

4 Adjust the **Reading view font size** to suit your preference according to the device you are using

Sharing Pages

When you want to share a web page of interest, Microsoft Edge provides the ability to share a link to that page's URL address or a screenshot of the part of that page visible in your browser:

Integrated sharing is a great new feature in Microsoft Edge on Windows 10.

 Click the **Share** button – to open the Share panel

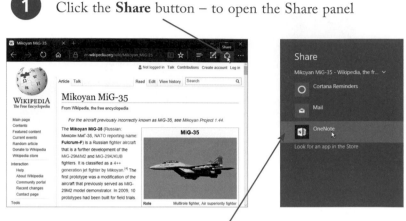

 Select the **OneNote** option on the Share panel

Sharing to the **Reading List** just saves the link by the name you give it.

 Add a note if desired, then click **Send** to share a hyperlink to the web page

Send ⊕

Mikoyan MiG-35 - Wikipedia, the free encyclopedia

Add a note

4 Open the OneNote app on any device to see the shared link

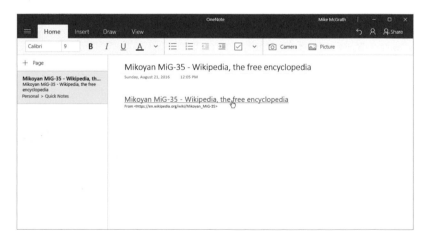

5 Returning to the web page, click the **Share** button again, then click the down arrow in the Share panel to reveal the drop-down options

You can share a screenshot to a printer app if you want to print it out.

6 Select the **Screenshot** option, then share to OneNote again

7 Choose the target notebook and **Add a note** if desired

8 Click **Send** to share the screenshot

9 Open the OneNote app on any device to see the screenshot

You can share to more services by installing the appropriate app from the Windows Store. For example, to share to Facebook, install the Facebook app.

Making Web Notes

Microsoft Edge lets you make notes and highlight important text directly onto web pages, creating your own "Web Notes" that can be saved and shared:

Web Notes are a great new feature in Microsoft Edge in Windows 10.

1 Open a page in Microsoft Edge, then click the Web Note button to switch to **Web Note** mode

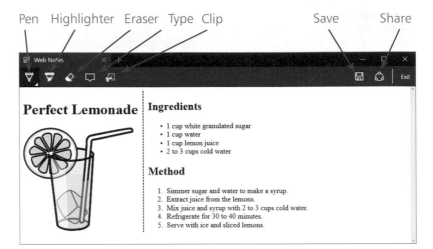

Pen   Highlighter   Eraser   Type   Clip   Save   Share

The **Clip** tool simply copies a selected area to the clipboard so you can paste it into another app, such as Paint.

2 Click the Pen icon to select the **Pen** tool, then choose a color and nib size

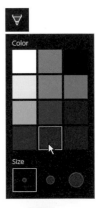

3 Now, use the cursor to scribble a note on the page using your chosen color and nib size

You can double-click the Eraser icon and select **Clear all ink** to remove highlighter and pen notes.

4 Click the **Eraser** icon, then drag the cursor across your note if you want to erase individual written characters

5 Click the **Highlighter** icon to select the Highlighter tool, then choose a color and shape

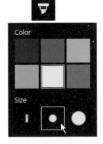

6 Now, use the cursor to highlight any items of particular importance

162

7 Click the **Type** icon, then click on the page at a point where you want to type a note

 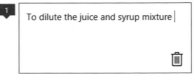

8 Enter text into the box that appears, to create a typed note

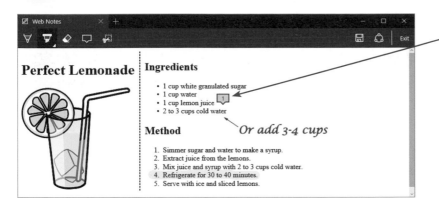

Click the numbered icon beside a typed note to collapse or expand that typed note.

9 Click the **Save** icon, then choose to save the complete noted page to **OneNote** – so it will be sent to OneDrive

10 Open the **OneNote** app on any device to see the page, complete with your notes

You can also save to your **Favorites** or **Reading List**, and use the **Share** button to send the noted page to another location.

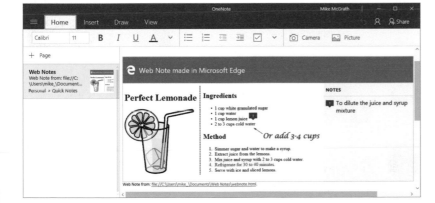

Ask Cortana

One of the great innovations in Windows 10 is the Personal Digital Assistant named "Cortana". This is an enhancement to the Search box feature that allows the user to search, and much more, by verbal communication once it has been enabled:

Cortana is new in Windows 10 but performance may vary by region. If Cortana is not working or enabled in your country, try setting your region to "United States" in Settings, Time & language > Region & language.

 Click in the Taskbar Search box then, when asked, enter your name and agree to allow access to your location

 Ensure your microphone is correctly configured, then click the microphone icon at the right of the Search box

3 Repeat the phrase that Cortana gives you, being sure to speak clearly without any background noise, then click **Next** to close

You can also click the microphone icon in the Search box to make Cortana begin listening.

4 Click the Search box to open the Cortana pane, then click the **Settings** button

5 Slide the **Hey Cortana** toggle button to the **On** position, and choose any other options you prefer

Cortana collects users' personal data to further personalize results, and as such is subject to child-protection laws. Therefore, the user must be at least 13 years of age (checked against age data in user profiles) or Cortana will refuse to answer questions.

 Upon completion of setup, just say "Hey Cortana" to make Cortana listen

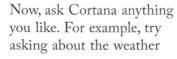 Now, ask Cortana anything you like. For example, try asking about the weather

The best way to learn Cortana commands is to simply try out different ways to phrase your question. Here are some Cortana commands that worked successfully when we tried them:

- **Cortana Search** – "Pink discography"

- **Cortana Calendar** – "Create a meeting with David"

- **Cortana Reminder** – "Remind me at 4pm"

- **Cortana Alarm** – "Wake me up in 2 hours"

- **Cortana Maps** – "Map of Washington DC"

- **Cortana Weather** – "What's the forecast this weekend"

- **Cortana Music** – "Play music", "Pause music", "Resume music"

- **Cortana Pictures** – "Show me a picture of Cortana"

- **Cortana App Launch** – "Open Command Prompt"

- **Cortana News** – "Show me today's news"

- **Cortana Finance** – "Microsoft Stock price"

- **Cortana Sports** – "New York Jets next game"

- **Cortana Fun** – "Sing me a song"

- **Cortana Note-taking** – "Take a note"

Cortana requires an internet connection so will be unable to answer if you should lose your Wi-Fi connection. More features will be added to Cortana in the future.

The ability to have Cortana take notes is a great new feature – the notes are automatically added to OneNote as audio files, so can be played back anywhere.

165

You can also control the **Zoom** function with the keyboard:

- **Ctrl** plus **+** (plus sign) = zoom in by 25%

- **Ctrl** plus **-** (minus sign) = zoom out by 25%

- **Ctrl** plus **0** = zoom to default 100%

Most web pages have headers and footers that print along with the page contents. Prevent this when printing web pages by setting the **Headers and footers** option to **Off** in the Print preview dialog.

The Windows 10 Anniversary update introduced support for browser extensions – try the Translator extension for non-English websites.

Miscellaneous Tips

Get in close
Microsoft Edge allows users to zoom in on a page for those sites where text is hard to read. Click the **...** (**More options**) button, then click the **+** or **-** buttons to select the **Zoom** level required.

Browse in private
Open a window in private browsing mode and your browser data (history, temporary internet files, and cookies) won't be saved. Click **...** (**More options**), then click **New InPrivate Window**.

Pin to Start
Pin the current web page to your Start menu as a tile that you can click to open, at any time in a new tabbed window. Click **...** (**More options**), then click **Pin this page to Start**.

Support for plugins
Microsoft Edge does not currently support plugins such as Java or Silverlight but you can switch to Internet Explorer for support. Click **...** (**More options**), then click **Open with Internet Explorer**.

Disable Flash
You may wish to disable Adobe Flash Player for security reasons. Click **...** (**More options**) > **Settings** > **View advanced settings**, then slide the **Use Adobe Flash Player** toggle button to **Off**.

Change the theme
Microsoft Edge offers an alternative to its default "Light" theme. Click **...** (**More options**) > **Settings**, then choose an option from the **Choose a theme** drop-down menu.

Provide a Home button
You can add a "Home" button on the Edge browser toolbar. Click **...** (**More options**) > **Settings** > **View advanced settings**, then slide the **Show the home button** toggle button to **On**.

See your Favorites
Websites saved into the "Favorites Bar" folder can be shown on the Microsoft Edge toolbar. Click **...** (**More options**) > **Settings**, then slide the **Show the favorites bar** toggle button to **On**.

Add extensions
You can add features to Microsoft Edge. Click **...** (**More options**) > **Extensions**, then select **Get extensions from the Store**.

12 Email

In this chapter, we look at
perhaps the most popular
PC application of all
– email. Learn how to
safeguard your messages
and account settings, how
to avoid spam and viruses,
plus much more.

Setting Up an Email Account

The **Mail** app is a new Universal Windows app in Windows 10. Advanced features may be added in the future.

Clicking the **Outlook 2016** item on the Start menu will only open the Welcome dialog if no accounts are set up. Once one or more email accounts are set up it will subsequently launch the app ready to read and write emails.

Unlike earlier predecessors, Windows 10 provides users with an email program called "Mail". This provides few configuration options for the more advanced email user. If this is you, you may wish to install a third-party program. Mozilla, author of the Firefox web browser, provides the free **Thunderbird** email client, while another free email program with a very good reputation is **Eudora**. These can both be downloaded from the manufacturers' websites. If you do an internet search, you will also find a multitude of other email programs. This might be a good time to try out a few and see how you get on with them. Alternatively, you can opt to stay with Microsoft. The **Outlook 2016** mail app is included with an Office 365 subscription.

The Outlook 2016 mail app
To set up a first email account on Outlook 2016:

 Click the **Outlook 2016** app item on the Start menu – to launch the "Welcome" dialog

 Click the **Next** button on the Welcome dialog – to open the **Add an Email Account** dialog

 You are asked "Do you want to set up Outlook to connect to an email account?" – choose **Yes**, then click **Next**

 If you already have an email account, choose **Email Account** and enter your account details, then click **Next**

Add Account

Auto Account Setup
Outlook can automatically configure many email accounts.

● **Email Account**

Your Name: Joanne Example
Example: Ellen Adams

Email Address: joanne-example@outlook.com
Example: ellen@contoso.com

Password: ********
Retype Password: ********
Type the password your Internet service provider has given you.

○ Manual setup or additional server types

< Back   Next >   Cancel

If you don't already have an email account, choose **Manual setup or additional server types** to establish new account details.

5 Next, enter your account details in the **Windows Security** dialog

6 Choose the **Remember my credentials** option if you want these to be retained, then click the **OK** button

Hot tip

Further email accounts can be added anytime with the **Outlook 2016** app's **+ Add account** button on the **File** > **Info** screen.

7 After configuration completes, click the **Finish** button – to launch the app so you can now send and receive email

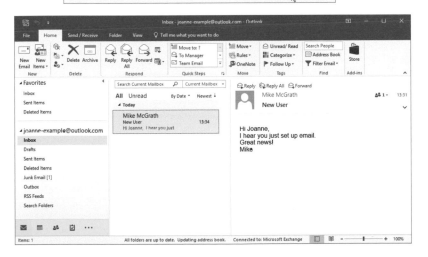

Don't forget

If you are likely to use **Outlook 2016** frequently, pin it to the **Start** menu or Taskbar.

Back Up Your Emails

The provision of email facilities is a very important function of the modern-day computer, and just as people often like to keep personal letters, they also like to keep their emails. It is also an important means of business communication and these messages usually need to be kept as records.

Outlook 2016 provides an easy way to back up your messages:

 On the Outlook 2016 menu choose **File** > **Open & Export** – to see the "Open" screen

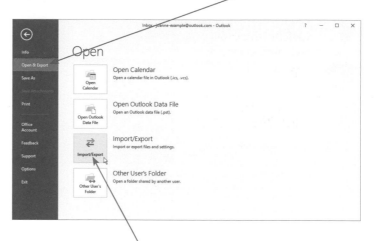

 Next, click the **Import/Export** button – to launch the "Import and Export Wizard" dialog

 Select the **Export to a file** option, then click **Next**

If you just want to back up a particular message, double-click it and select **Save As** from the **File** menu. You can then save it where you like.

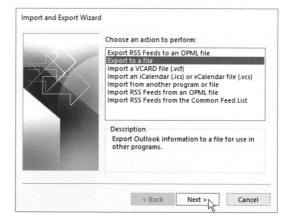

4 Now, select the compact **Outlook Data File (.pst)** file type (or **Comma Separated Values** for a text version), then click **Next**

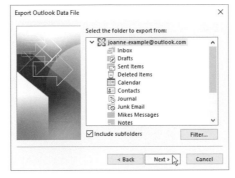

Comma Separated Values files can usefully allow you to import messages into an Excel worksheet.

5 Select the folder you wish to back up, or choose your account to back up everything, then click **Next**

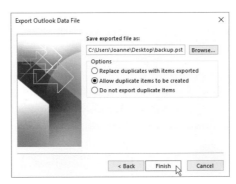

Choosing to back up everything will also export junk mail. Choose only what you really need to back up.

171

6 Choose a file destination and select a duplication option, then click **Finish**

7 Enter a password if required, then click **OK** to create the backup file of your chosen file type

backup.pst   backup.csv

To restore your account, simply reverse the procedure by choosing **Import from another program or file** in Step 3, then browse to your backup file.

Open Blocked Attachments

Viruses transmitted by email are almost always contained in an attachment to the email. However, the attachment must be opened by the user before the virus can be released.

To prevent this, Outlook 2016 has a virus protection feature which prevents any attachment that it considers unsafe from being opened. When this happens, you will see a message at the top of the email saying that access to the attachment has been blocked. An example of this is shown below:

Outlook 2016 can be configured to read email in plain text format. When you enable this setting, no dangerous content in the email is run. Do it as follows:

• From the **File** menu, click **Options** > **Mail**

• Choose the **Trust Center** option, then click the **Trust Center Settings** button

• Choose **Email Security**, then check the **Read all standard mail in plain text** option

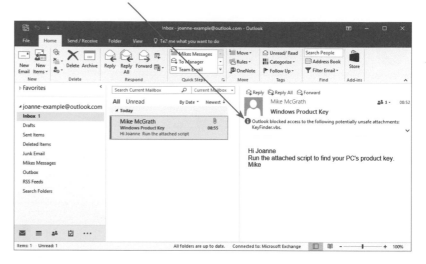

This is all very well, and the feature will prevent people opening dangerous attachments, either through ignorance or carelessness. However, if you are certain that an attachment is safe – you recognize the sender and know exactly what the attachment is, for example – you may wish to know how to open it:

1 Ensure that the Outlook 2016 app is closed

2 In Windows Search box on the Taskbar, enter "regedit" then click **Run command** – to launch the Registry Editor

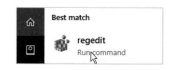

3 Next, navigate to this registry key
HKEY_CURRENT_USER\SOFTWARE\Microsoft\Office\16.0\Outlook\Security

Some email providers, such as **Gmail**, prohibit the sender from attaching files that have unsafe file extensions, in an attempt to reduce the spread of malware.

4 Right-click in the right pane and choose **New > String value**, then precisely name the value as **Level1Remove**

5 Double-click on the new value to open the "Edit String" dialog and enter the file extension (including a period) of the blocked file you want to open, for example **.vbs**

173

6 Click **OK** to close the Edit String dialog, then close the Registry Editor

7 Open the Outlook 2016 app and see that access to the attached file is no longer blocked

8 Click on the attachment and choose **Save to Disk...** in the Warning dialog, then locate the file to freely open it

9 Close Outlook 2016 then reopen the Registry Editor and delete the **Level1Remove** value – to resume blocking

High-Risk File Attachments

An email attachment ending in any of the file extensions in the table below can, potentially, be carrying a virus:

Note that in general, image formats are considered to be safe. The exception to this is the **JPEG** format, which can carry a virus.

The extension of a malware file may have been changed in order to disguise it. Be wary of all attachments from unknown sources.

File Extension	Description
.ADE	Microsoft Access Project extension
.ADP	Microsoft Access Project
.BAS	Visual Basic Class module
.BAT	Batch file
.CHM	Compiled HTML help file
.CMD	Windows NT Command Script
.COM	MS-DOS application
.CPL	Control Panel extension
.CRT	Security certificate
.EXE	Application
.HLP	Windows help file
.HTA	HTML application
.INF	Setup information file
.INS	Internet communication settings
.ISP	Internet communication settings
.JS	JScript file
.JSE	JScript Encoded Script file
.LNK	Shortcut
.MDB	Microsoft Access application
.MDE	Microsoft Access MDE database
.MSC	Microsoft Common Console document
.MSI	Windows installer package
.MSP	Windows installer patch
.MST	Visual Test Source file
.PCD	Photo CD image
.PIF	Shortcut to MS-DOS program
.REG	Registry file
.SCR	Screensaver
.SCT	Windows Script Component
.URL	Internet shortcut
.VB	Visual Basic file
.VBE	VBScript Encoded Script file
.VBS	VBScript Script file
.ZIP	Zipped folder

Low-Risk File Attachments

The file types in this table are extremely unlikely to be carrying a virus and can be considered to be safe:

File Extension	Description
.GIF	Picture – Graphics Interchange Format
.TIF or .TIFF	Picture – Tagged Image File Format
.MPEG	Movie – Motion Picture Expert Group
.AVI	Movie – Audio Video Interleaved
.MP3	Sound – MPEG compressed audio
.WAV	Sound – Audio
.TXT or .TEXT	Notepad document
.BMP	Picture – Windows Bitmap
.ICO	Picture – Icon
.PNG	Picture – Portable Network Graphic
.WMF	Picture – Windows Meta File
.LOG	Log file

In an effort to disguise the extension of the file in which the virus is hidden, some virus writers give the file two extensions. The dangerous one is always the last. If you ever get such an attachment, delete it immediately.

Open Blocked Images

Another security feature in **Outlook 2016** prevents the automatic download of images within emails which have been included from web pages. In this event, areas in the email message that contain images display a red X placeholder rather than the image:

> ☒ Right-click or tap and hold here to download pictures. To help protect your privacy, Outlook prevented automatic download of this picture from the Internet.

An attachment extension to be particularly wary of is **.ZIP**. This catches many people out, as most PC users are familiar with the Zip compression format and see no threat in it.

This protects the user from potentially offensive material and helps to prevent spam. Many spammers include an image URL in their emails that notifies the spammer when the message is opened – confirming that the address is real.

Should the user wish to see the image, they just have to right-click and choose **Download Pictures**. It is also possible to disable the feature in **Outlook 2016** so that all images are shown automatically when the message is opened. Do this by clicking **File > Options** then choose **Trust Center**. Click the **Trust Center Settings** button, then choose the **Automatic Download** item in the left pane. Now, uncheck the option **Don't download pictures automatically in HTML email or RSS items**.

Manage Senders

Most email apps provide the ability to create a list of "safe senders" whose incoming messages you consider trustworthy. Conversely, they also typically let you create a list of "blocked senders", who are deemed untrustworthy. Creating a safe sender list and a blocked sender list helps ensure that a message will not be incorrectly marked as spam when it arrives.

In Outlook 2016 for example, the Junk email filter automatically moves suspicious messages to the **Junk Email** folder. Unless you check this regularly, you may fail to notice it has incorrectly moved a message there from a reliable source. Adding that source to the app's **Safe Senders** list would prevent that from happening:

Hot tip

If you receive emails from various trusted sources at the same domain, say people within the same company domain, you can elect to add the entire domain to the Safe Senders list by choosing **Never Block Sender's Domain** on the Junk menu.

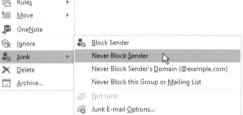

1 Right-click on any message in your mailbox that you have received from a trusted source, then choose **Junk > Never Block Sender** – to add that source to your Safe Senders list

2 Click **OK** to close a dialog that confirms the addition

3 Next, on the Home tab click **Junk > Junk E-mail Options...** – to launch the Junk Email Options dialog

Don't forget

Email addresses and domains in the **Safe Senders** list are never treated as Junk email.

4 Choose the **Safe Senders** tab to see the trusted source has now been added to the list

Hot tip

You can also use this **Add...** button to manually add the email addresses of trusted sources to the Safe Senders list.

Hot tip

Check these options if you want to add sources to the Safe Senders list from your Contacts list, and people to whom you send messages.

5 Now, choose the **Options** tab, then if you want to restrict incoming messages to strictly only sources on your **Safe Senders** list, check the **Safe Lists Only** option

Don't forget

You can select the **Blocked Senders** tab on the Junk Email Options dialog to create a list of email addresses you do not trust.

6 Click **Apply** to implement the option, then click **OK** to close the dialog

177

A Spam-Free Inbox

Spam accounts for approximately three-quarters of email traffic worldwide. That adds up to several billion emails every day.

If you find yourself the recipient of an endless stream of advertisements, too-good-to-be-true offers, etc., what can you do about it?

The first step is to close your account and then set up a new one – this will stop spam immediately. You then need to make sure the new account is kept out of the spammers' reach. Observing the following rules will help:

- Make your address as long as possible. Among other things, spammers use automated generators that churn out millions of combinations (aaa@aol.com, aab@aol.com, and so on). It won't take them long to catch up with bob@aol.com.

- Never post your address on a website. Spammers use spiders that trawl the web looking for the @ symbol, which is in all email addresses.

- If you need to give an address to access a web page, give a false one. Alternatively, set up a specific account with filters that direct all received emails to the deleted items folder. Use this account when an address is asked for.

- Never click the "Unsubscribe from this mailing list" link in a received spam email. This tells the spammer that your address is real and could open the floodgates.

- Make use of your email program's filters (Rules in Outlook 2016). Properly configured, these can cut out a lot of spam.

- Use a Bayesian filter. This is available as a third-party product and integrates with your email program. Its effectiveness is due to the fact that it is "intelligent", and thus can be trained in much in the same way as Voice Recognition software.

  The Bayesian filter examines all aspects of a message, as opposed to simple keyword checking that classifies a message as spam on the basis of a single word or phrase. Once set up and trained, a Bayesian filter will eliminate 99% of spam.

Once you are on the spammers' lists, the only way of stopping them is to close the account.

Never reply to a spammer. If you do, you will confirm that your address is a real one.

Chatrooms, Newsgroups and Message Boards are favorite places for spammers. Never post your email address on these websites.

Organize Your Emails

If you're like most people, your Inbox will be bulging at the seams with messages from weeks, months and even years ago. This tip shows how to tidy it up and then keep it tidy:

 Create a new message folder for each of your contacts

 Go through the Inbox and move your messages to the new categorized folders. Delete any you don't want

Having created order out of chaos, you need to make sure it stays that way, and without having to do it manually. To this end, you now need to set up your email program's message filters to do the job automatically:

 On the Outlook 2016 Ribbon, click the Home tab, then select **Rules** > **Manage Rules & Alerts** > **New Rule** – to launch the "Rules Wizard" dialog

4 Choose **Move messages from someone to a folder**

5 Click the **from** item link – to open a dialog where you can select a contact

6 Click the **move it to** item link – to open a dialog where you can select a folder

Rules Wizard

Start from a template or from a blank rule
Step 1: Select a template
Stay Organized
Move messages from someone to a folder
Move messages with specific words in the subject to a folder
Move messages sent to a public group to a folder
Flag messages from someone for follow-up
Move RSS items from a specific RSS Feed to a folder
Stay Up to Date
Display mail from someone in the New Item Alert Window
Play a sound when I get messages from someone
Send an alert to my mobile device when I get messages from someone
Start from a blank rule
Apply rule on messages I receive
Apply rule on messages I send

Step 2: Edit the rule description (click an underlined value)
Apply this rule after the message arrives
from Mike McGrath
move it to the Mikes Messages folder
and stop processing more rules

Example: Move mail from my manager to my High Importance folder

Cancel   < Back   Next >   Finish

7 Click **Finish**, **OK**, and from this point on all messages from the specified contact will be moved automatically to the specified folder

A big advantage of organizing your emails in this way is found when you need to locate an old message for re-reading. Instead of having to search through an over-flowing Inbox, you will know exactly where it is.

You can create multiple email rules but you should be aware that their order is significant. Rules are processed in the order listed – a rule may be overridden by a subsequent rule.

Automatic Picture Resizing

As anybody who regularly uses email will know, email programs allow users to either insert images directly into the email or attach them as a file.

The problem with this is that unless the image has been reduced in size in an imaging program (a process of which many people are unsure), it is possible to end up sending a huge picture file that will take the recipient ages to download. Most people find this extremely irritating, as it can occupy their connection for a considerable length of time. This is particularly so if they use a dial-up connection.

Windows saves the day with its Email Picture Resizing utility:

1 Right-click the image you want to send with your email, select **Send to** and then **Mail Recipient**

Attach Files	— ☐ ✕

Picture size: Original Size ⌄

Smaller: 640 x 480
Small: 800 x 600
Medium: 1024 x 768
Large: 1280 x 1024
Original Size

Attach   Cancel

2 Select the required option, e.g. **Small, Medium, Original Size**, etc., and then click **Attach**

3 Click **OK** and an email message window will open with the resized image attached. All you have to do is type in the address and the text before sending the message

A couple of things to be aware of:

● Pictures resized in this way are converted to the **JPEG** format, which you may or may not want.

● Some image formats (Photoshop's **PSD**, for example) cannot be converted by the utility, and thus cannot be resized – they will be attached to the email but at the original size.

Don't forget

You can resize any number of pictures at the same time – you are not restricted to just one.

Beware

Be wary of using the **Small** and **Smaller** resize options. While these reduce the size of files enormously, they also reduce the quality of the images considerably.

Hot tip

Be aware of file formats, as they also determine the size of an image file. For example, a **BMP** file of 4MB may be reduced to 100KB in **JPEG** format!

13 Multimedia

Multimedia has always been one of the most popular uses of PCs. Here, we look at various ways of enhancing your multimedia experience, and show you some recommended software.

Play any Media File

Video and audio files in their raw state are huge in size, so compression techniques are used to reduce their size for downloading and copying. The program that does the compressing is known as a codec (**co**mpressor-**dec**ompressor) and there are lots of them. Two well-known examples are **DIVX** for video and **MP3** for audio. Once a file has been compressed, it must then be decompressed before it can be played. The decompression is done by the same codec that compressed the file originally. This can create a problem for computer users if they have a media file but are unable to play it because the required codec is not installed on their PC. There are a couple of ways to resolve this issue:

● Check the file with a program that will analyze it and tell you which codec is required to play it, e.g. **GSpot** – see page 201.

● Install a codec pack, which contains codecs for virtually all types of media file.

Windows 10 provides most commonly-used codecs, but there are still many others. There are several codec packs available on the internet, and if you choose this option we suggest you do a bit of research before installing one. Some of them can cause more problems than they solve. One codec pack that we have evaluated and can recommend is the free **Shark007** codec pack, available for download at **shark007.net**

This application does just what it says – it installs all the codecs you are ever likely to need, without also installing superfluous features, such as bundled media players, etc.

Most of the codec packs are designed for specific versions of Windows. If you do decide to install one, be sure it is compatible with the Windows version you are using. **Shark007** say their "codecs are fully tested and supported for Windows 10".

There are two codec packs available from **Shark007** – one for the "Standard" codecs, and the other for "Advanced" codecs. We installed the **Advanced** pack for greater codec support.

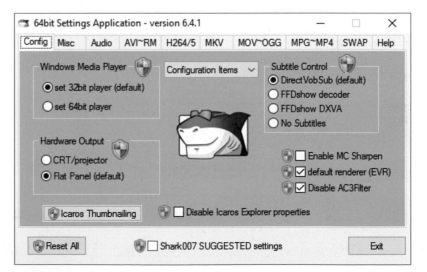

Multimedia Viewers

For viewing your pictures, Windows 10 provides the **Photos** app, which has a limited set of features. The powerful **IrfanView** imaging program has a vast range of features and is available free at **irfanview.com** – no computer user should be without it.

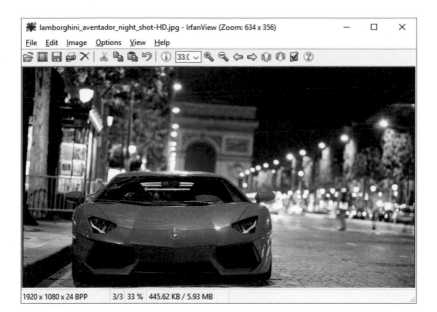

The **Photos** app is a new Universal Windows app in Windows 10 – expect more features to be added in the future.

IrfanView has a wide range of functions that can be further extended by downloading free plug-ins from the manufacturer's website.

For viewing video, Windows 10 provides the excellent **Windows Media Player** that has a good range of features but cannot play DVDs. The powerful **Zoom Player**, has an uncluttered interface and is available free at **inmatrix.com** – an unbeatable free app.

IrfanView and **Zoom Player** are both completely free of spyware and adware.

Game Play Optimization

The average computer system is not specified highly enough to play many of today's 3D games at their optimum level. By this, we mean all sound/graphic enhancements and features turned on and set at maximum. With "all guns blazing" most PCs will struggle, with gameplay being slow and jerky.

The following tips will help to prevent this:

- Reinstall the game and choose the option that installs the majority (or all) of the game's data on the hard drive. The less the game has to access the disc, the more smoothly it will run.

- Before you start the game, switch the PC off for a few seconds. Doing this will clear the memory and ensure the PC is in an optimal condition.

- When playing the game, make sure no other applications are running on the PC.

- Try reducing the amount of action, e.g. reduce the number of opponents, cars in a racing game, etc. The less that is going on, the better the PC will be able to cope with the game.

- Go into the game's graphics setup options and reduce the screen resolution. Then, reduce settings such as Anti-Aliasing, Shadows, and Textures. These features improve graphic quality considerably but do place a heavy load on the PC.

Before buying any 3D game, make sure your CPU and memory match the recommended system requirements on its box. You must also have the version of DirectX required by the game, otherwise it won't run properly, if at all.

If the game's installation options allow you to install the entire game to the hard drive, do so. Having to constantly retrieve data from the CD/DVD drive can cause the game to stutter.

Achieving a smooth level of gameplay is usually a compromise between graphics quality and performance, requiring some trial and error.

Controls	Audio	Display	Graphics	Game

Video Mode — 1920 x 1080 (60 Hz) — Affects video memory and GPU performance.
Aspect Ratio — Auto
Texture Quality — High
Reflection Resolution — Very High
Water Quality — High
Shadow Quality — Very High
Texture Filter Quality — Highest
View Distance — 100
Detail Distance — 100
Vehicle Density — 100
Shadow Density — 16
Definition — Off
VSync — Off
Auto Configure
Benchmark

Warning: Your graphics settings are near, or exceed, the suggested resource limits for your system. It is recommended that you reduce your graphics settings in order to run the game optimally.

Resource Usage — 1588 / 992 MB

- The final and most drastic option is to upgrade your system's hardware, i.e. the memory, and possibly the CPU and video system as well.

Keep the Discs in the Drawer

One of the most irritating things about playing games on a computer is the constant need to insert and change discs. This can also be the eventual cause of physical damage to the discs.

While most game manufacturers allow their games to be run directly from the hard drive, thus eliminating the need to use the discs, there are still some that don't. Some people try to get round this by copying the disc to the hard drive and then installing the game from there. Unfortunately, this rarely works – when you try to run the game you usually get a "No disk in CD drive" error message. This is the manufacturers' copy protection at work.

The solution to this problem is a virtual drive. This is an emulated drive created and controlled by software. The user creates an image of the game's disc on the hard drive, which can be played in the virtual drive – the real disc is not required at all.

There are many of these applications available on the internet. A good one is **Virtual CD**, available at **www.virtualcd-online.com** You can either buy the full version or try out a trial version:

Virtual drives can be used with any type of program – they are not restricted to games. Although most applications now offer an "install to disk" option, there are still many that do not. A virtual drive is the answer.

185

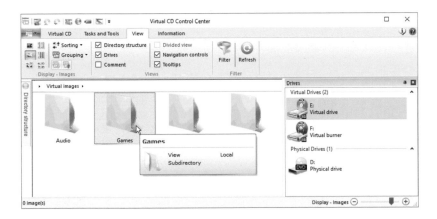

Virtual drive programs can create up to 23 virtual drives, which means you can have up to 23 different games pre-loaded and ready to go. You can put the discs in a drawer and forget about them. Also, as the games are being played from the hard drive, they will perform better.

Another advantage of these programs is that they can override most manufacturers' copy protection methods.

Most CD/DVD-authoring programs also provide a virtual CD drive. With these, though, you will only have one drive.

Home Media Streaming

Anything that you can play in Windows Media Player, you can share with other computers and devices on your home network. For example, sharing music between a laptop and a desktop PC:

This tip requires your home network to be set up, and both devices to be part of the HomeGroup.

These are the default shared libraries for the HomeGroup but you can choose which libraries to share when joining, or change your choice later.

You may have to wait a few moments as the list of contents is transferred from the other computer.

Contacting the remote media library ...
Cancel

1 Open Windows Media Player on the laptop, then select the **Library** view and click the **Stream** button

2 Next check all of the top three items to allow the laptop's Windows Media Player to have access to **Other Libraries** – the

media libraries that were agreed to be shared by a desktop PC on your network when it joined the HomeGroup

3 Under **Other Libraries** in the laptop's Windows Media Player, expand the desktop PC's shared media libraries to discover what is being shared – in this case, see **Music**, **Video**, **Pictures**, and **Recorded TV** libraries

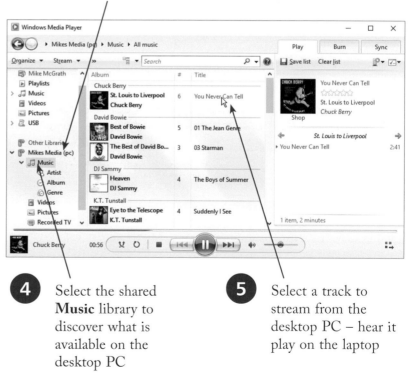

4 Select the shared **Music** library to discover what is available on the desktop PC

5 Select a track to stream from the desktop PC – hear it play on the laptop

...cont'd

You can stream from a laptop to a desktop PC on your network:

 Start by turning on the desktop PC, and start Windows
Media Player on it

 Open Windows Media Player on the laptop and drag a
track from your Music onto the **Playlist**

3 Hit the **Pause** button to stop playback on your laptop

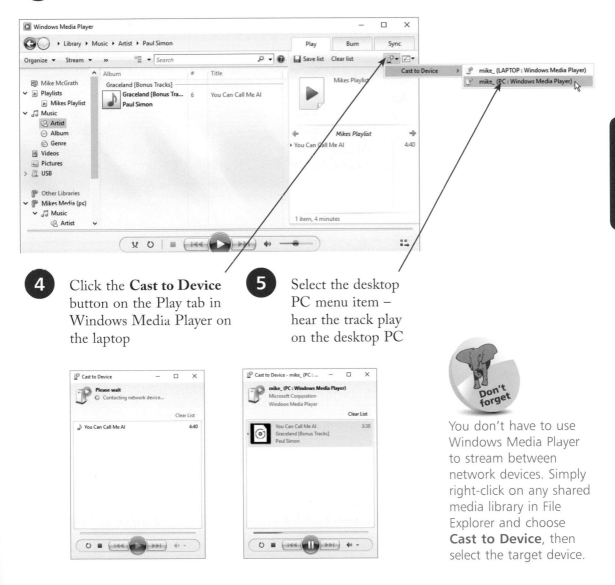

4 Click the **Cast to Device** button on the Play tab in Windows Media Player on the laptop

5 Select the desktop PC menu item – hear the track play on the desktop PC

Don't forget

You don't have to use Windows Media Player to stream between network devices. Simply right-click on any shared media library in File Explorer and choose **Cast to Device**, then select the target device.

Streaming Xbox Media

The Xbox app is a great new Universal Windows app on Windows 10 that brings Xbox gaming to your PC.

You must sign in to both the Xbox console and Xbox app using the same Microsoft Account.

The first time you run this program, you may see the Get Started setup. Select **Express** for the recommended options, or **Custom** to personalize the settings.

If you have an Xbox One console on the same network, you can stream games, video and music to your PC:

 Turn on your Xbox console and controller, then sign in using your Microsoft Account

 On your PC, launch the Xbox app from the Start menu then sign in using the same Microsoft Account

 Click the **Connection** button in the left-hand toolbar when there is a green dot to show that your Xbox is recognized

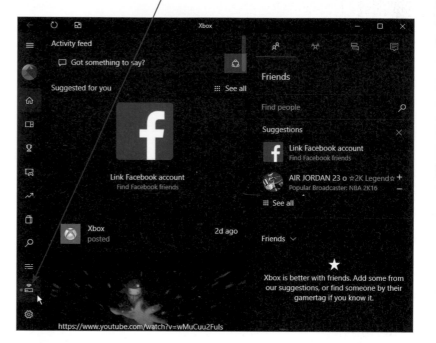

 Select the Xbox console to connect, if more than one is listed, then click the **Stream** link

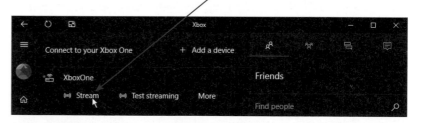

5 Your Xbox console screen now loads in the Xbox app and is displayed full screen

Groove Music is an Xbox subscription service but you can try it free on a limited-time trial basis.

6 Connect an Xbox controller to your PC using a USB to micro-USB cable, so you can interact with the Xbox app

7 Use the Xbox controller to play an app or game on your PC – just like on your Xbox

To use a wireless Xbox controller after using it on your PC you will have to re-sync the controller, using the console's sync button or a USB cable.

Graphic Formats Unraveled

When using graphics files in documents, presentations, web pages, or for printing, it is important that you choose a format that is suitable for the task in hand. Using the wrong one can result in poor-quality images, images that take an eternity to open, or images with unnecessarily high file sizes.

The first thing to realize is that image formats are split into two main groups: Vector and Raster.

Vector

Vector images are composed of mathematically-defined geometric shapes, e.g. lines, squares, circles, etc. and are typically generated by drawing applications such as Adobe Illustrator and Microsoft Visio. Two notable advantages of this format are:

- Image size can be increased to an almost unlimited degree without noticeable loss of image quality.

- Individual parts of an image can be edited. For example, if a particular image contains both text and objects, it is possible to change the text's formatting – font, color, size, etc.

Vector formats tend to be proprietary, i.e. specific to a particular program. However, many drawing applications allow you to save an image in formats used by other popular vector programs.

Commonly-used vector formats include:

- **WMF** – this is the standard vector file used in Microsoft products, such as Microsoft Office.

- **PCT** – this is the standard vector format used by Apple Mac operating systems.

- **EPS** – this format can be used on a variety of platforms, including Apple Mac and Windows.

- **AI** – this format is the default used by the industry standard Adobe Illustrator vector graphics drawing application.

Raster

In raster files, the image is comprised of a grid, or matrix, of tiny squares called pixels. This allows extremely complex pictures to be recorded, typically photographs, and it's this characteristic that makes them the most widely-used format.

Many of the vector formats (including the four mentioned on the right), can also handle raster data. These are often called "MetaFiles", such as the Windows MetaFile format WMF.

You may also encounter the **SVG** (Scalable Vector Graphic) file format. This enables two-dimensional vector images to be displayed in web pages using **XML** (eXtensible Markup Language).

The main drawback is that in their raw state, raster files can be very large. However, this is compensated for by the fact that this format can be heavily compressed to reduce file size.

With regard to compression, there are two types, lossy and lossless:

- **Lossy** – with this method, unnecessary data is permanently stripped out of the file, thus reducing its size. Although it may be imperceptible, the quality of the image is reduced.

- **Lossless** – here, data is temporarily removed from the file. When the file is opened, the data is replaced. Thus, there is no loss of image quality.

Commonly-used raster formats are:

- **JPEG** – a lossy format, JPEG's main advantage is the fact that it can be highly compressed. This makes it ideal for use in web pages, and where a low file size is required. It can also handle 24-bit color, and so can be used for professional printing (although there are better formats for this).

- **GIF** – this is a low-size lossless image format, which is mostly found on websites where it is used for small low-quality images, such as advertising banners, clip art, etc. Use this format if you want the lowest possible file size and the quality of the image is not important.

- **PNG** – this is an advanced version of the GIF format and it offers several advantages, such as better color support and compression. PNGs are lossless.

- **TIFF** – this is a lossless format offering features that make it the ideal format for professional printing. File sizes are high but image quality is excellent.

Summary
For web pages where quality is not important, or low file size is, use GIF or PNG. Otherwise, use JPEG (a.k.a. JPG).

For general computer use, e.g. storing and viewing your holiday snaps, JPEG is the recommended format.

For professional printing of photographs, use the TIFF format.

There are several variants of the JPEG format. These include: JP2000, JPM, and JP3D. These are designed for more specific uses, such as volumetric imaging (JP3D), and usually require a plug-in.

191

If an image contains both drawing objects (vector) and photographs (raster), use a metafile format such as EPS.

Editing Your Photos

Calibrate the monitor
The first thing you must do is calibrate the monitor. If it is incorrectly set up, no matter how carefully you edit your images, when you print them, or view them on a different monitor, they will look different. You may even make them worse. Calibration software should be bundled with your monitor. If not, use the calibration utility provided by Windows – see page 136.

Convert the image to a Lossless format
As we saw on page 191, image formats are either lossy or lossless. Every time a lossy image is edited, some loss of image data occurs. Thus, the more times it is edited, the worse the end result. Lossless images, on the other hand, can be edited any number of times with no loss of quality. So, before you edit any image of the lossy type, convert it to a **TIFF**, which is lossless. Having edited the image, convert it back to the original file type. It takes a few seconds and ensures that the original image quality is retained.

Brightness and Contrast adjustments
All image editors provide brightness and contrast controls. Many also have an auto one-click setting that does the job automatically. While both can work well, often the result is less than optimal.

A better and more reliable way is to use the image editor's **Histogram** control. This presents a graphical representation of the image showing its color distribution in terms of brightness and darkness. The left of the graph represents black and the right represents white.

Consider the following example of a badly under-exposed picture:

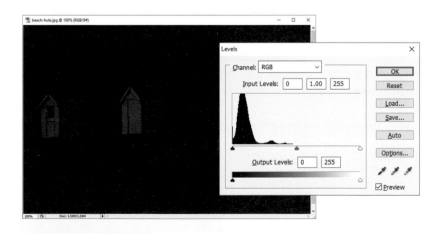

Hot tip

If you have an image that cannot be replaced, make a copy and use that for editing. If you mess it up, you've still got the original.

Don't forget

Before you edit a photo, convert it to a TIFF file first. This can be done with the editing program. Then, reopen it to start editing.

Hot tip

The imaging program provided by Windows is Windows Photo Viewer. Unfortunately, it doesn't provide any editing features. If you're serious about your photos, we suggest you acquire a more capable imaging program.

...cont'd

The image's **Histogram** shows that its data is over to the left of the graph, i.e. its dark tones are overemphasized. (If an image's exposure is correct, the data will be centered in the graph.)

 Drag the white pointer to where the data begins – to set the image's exposure to the correct level

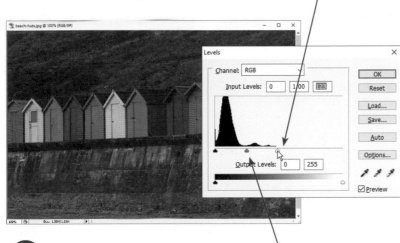

 Now, drag the gray pointer in the middle – to set the image's contrast to the correct level

Color Correction

The next adjustment to make is to the image's colors. This is done with the **Hue/Saturation** control (shown below). A common mistake is to adjust all the colors simultaneously until the picture "looks about right". However, this often results in one color being correct and the others being incorrect.

The right pointer controls light tones (highlights), the left one controls dark tones (shadows), and the middle one controls midtones (contrast).

If an image is over-exposed, its data will be to the right of the graph. In this case, you would drag the black slider to where the data begins.

The right way to do it is to edit each color individually by selecting it from the **Edit** menu. Adjustments will thus affect that color only.

An example is shown on the next page.

Another more advanced tool that can be used for color correction is the Curves tool.

193

...cont'd

In this image, the grass and foliage have a yellowish tint that gives a slightly washed-out or faded look

Adjusting green only gives the grass and foliage a richer color, while the other colors remain unchanged

Color Cast Correction

A common problem with digital photos is the image having an unwanted tint. This can also be corrected with the **Hue/ Saturation** control. Select the color of the cast in the Edit menu and then drag the slider back to eliminate it.

Sharpening

The first rule of image sharpening is that this process is the last edit to be made. The second rule is to ignore the **Sharpen** and **Sharpen More** tools, as they provide little user control and usually result in the image being sharpened incorrectly.

The tool you should use is the **Unsharp Mask**. When using this, you need to zoom in closely so that you can work with precision.

Many imaging programs provide a zoom-in preview window for this purpose. If yours doesn't, use the program's zoom control to get in close.

The rule of thumb is to look for halos along sharp edges. When you see these, reduce the **Threshold** setting until the halos disappear, then you should be about right.

14 Miscellaneous

This chapter contains a number of tips that relate to both the PC and the internet. For example, how to store your data in the cloud and sync that data across all of your devices. We also look at some handy applications that may not be apparent at first glance.

Keyboard Calculator

Don't forget

Click the "hamburger" button to switch the **Calculator** app into **Scientific** mode, **Programmer** mode, **Date calculation** mode, or one of its many **Converter** modes.

The Calculator provided by Windows is a very handy and much-used application. However, operating it with a mouse is less than ideal as it is very easy to press the wrong button. You could never add up a column of figures at anything like the speed of a real calculator.

The tip described below allows you to do just that:

1 Press the **Num Lock** key on the keyboard to activate the numeric keypad

2 Type "calc" into the Taskbar Search box, then hit **Enter** to launch the **Calculator** app

Calculator					– □ ×
≡ STANDARD				History Memory	

3.14159265

				96 + 6 =
				102
MC	MR	M+	M-	MS
				90 + 6 =
%	√	x^2	¹/ₓ	**96**
CE	C	⌫	÷	84 + 6 =
				90
7	8	9	×	
4	5	6	–	78 + 6 =
				84
1	2	3	+	
±	0	.	=	🗑

3 Instead of fiddling about with the mouse to enter numbers, simply use the numeric keypad on the right-hand side of the keyboard

Hot tip

Key	Action
/	The equivalent of divide
*	The equivalent of multiply
+	The equivalent of plus
-	The equivalent of minus
Enter	The equivalent of equals

Restart Windows Explorer

From time to time Windows Explorer, which is the application responsible for the Taskbar and the Desktop, will crash. The result is that the Taskbar and all the desktop icons will disappear, leaving a blank screen. With nothing to click, the user seemingly has no options with which to recover.

The solution is as follows:

 1 Press **Ctrl + Shift + Esc**. This opens the **Task Manager**

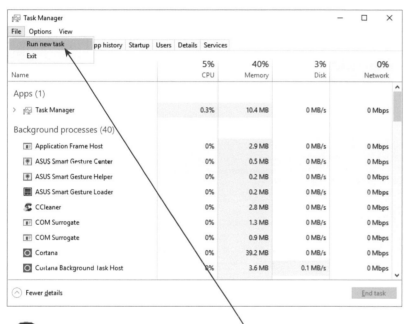

You can click the **Performance** tab in **Task Manager** to see usage graphs for your CPU, Memory, Disk, Ethernet, and Wi-Fi.

2 From the **File** menu, click **Run new task**

3 In the **Open** box, type "explorer" and then click **OK**

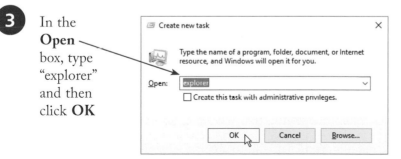

Windows will now restart Windows **Explorer**, which will in turn reinstate the Taskbar and the desktop icons.

If a process has "gone rogue", slowing down your PC to a crawl, open **Task Manager** then check the **Processes** > **CPU** column to select the wayward process and click **End task** to kill that process.

197

Turbo-Charge the Mouse

Many users are not aware that there are several aspects of the mouse that can be enhanced, both visually and operationally.

Pointer speed

The first is the speed at which the pointer moves across the screen. The default setting is fine for most users but some, gamers for example, will benefit from a faster speed:

 1 Go to **Control Panel** and click **Mouse**. Then click the **Pointer Options** tab

The **Pointers** tab provides a range of mouse pointers that you may find more suitable for your use of the PC than the default pointer.

The **Wheel** tab provides options to adjust horizontal and vertical scrolling actions with the mouse wheel.

Mouse Properties ✕

Buttons | Pointers | Pointer Options | Wheel | Hardware

Motion
Select a pointer speed:
Slow ——————◻—— Fast
☑ Enhance pointer precision

Snap To
◻ Automatically move pointer to the default button in a dialog box

Visibility
◻ Display pointer trails
Short ————————— Long
☑ Hide pointer while typing
◻ Show location of pointer when I press the CTRL key

OK | Cancel | Apply

 2 Drag the slider forward, click Apply then OK to increase the pointer's speed

Mouse Snap To

While you have the **Pointer Options** dialog box open, you can alter another setting that will change the mouse's behavior.

Enabling **Snap To** will, to a certain extent, eliminate the need to move your mouse, by making the pointer jump automatically to the default button whenever a new dialog box is opened. Some people love this; others hate it. Give it a try.

Have you ever been in a situation where you have simply lost the pointer? Checking **Show location of pointer when I press the CTRL key** will enable you to find it instantly the next time you lose it.

Easy Reading

The **ClearType** feature, which was originally introduced in Windows XP, is an anti-aliasing technique that smoothes the edges of fonts, thus making them easier to read.

With XP, the feature was disabled by default; with Windows 10 the default setting is on. However, not many users are aware that they can tweak the level of **ClearType**. This can be done as described below.

1 Go to **Control Panel** > **Display**. On the left, click **Adjust ClearType text** – to open the **ClearType Text Tuner**

2 At the first screen, click **Next**. At the second, select the monitor to apply the settings to (assuming you have more than one)

3 The next four screens will present you with different **ClearType** options

Not everybody likes **ClearType**. If you want to disable it, uncheck **Turn on ClearType** on the first screen.

You can also open the **ClearType Text Tuner** from the Run box with the "cttune" command.

ClearType Text Tuner   ✕

← 🅰 ClearType Text Tuner

Click the text sample that looks best to you (2 of 5)

The Quick Brown Fox Jumps Over the Lazy Dog. Lorem ipsum dolor sit amet, consectetuer adipiscing elit. Mauris ornare odio vel risus. Maecenas elit metus, pellentesque quis, pretium.	The Quick Brown Fox Jumps Over the Lazy Dog. Lorem ipsum dolor sit amet, consectetuer adipiscing elit. Mauris ornare odio vel risus. Maecenas elit metus, pellentesque quis, pretium.	The Quick Brown Fox Jumps Over the Lazy Dog. Lorem ipsum dolor sit amet, consectetuer adipiscing elit. Mauris ornare odio vel risus. Maecenas elit metus, pellentesque quis, pretium.
The Quick Brown Fox Jumps Over the Lazy Dog. Lorem ipsum dolor sit amet, consectetuer adipiscing elit. Mauris ornare odio vel risus. Maecenas elit metus, pellentesque quis, pretium.	The Quick Brown Fox Jumps Over the Lazy Dog. Lorem ipsum dolor sit amet, consectetuer adipiscing elit. Mauris ornare odio vel risus. Maecenas elit metus, pellentesque quis, pretium.	The Quick Brown Fox Jumps Over the Lazy Dog. Lorem ipsum dolor sit amet, consectetuer adipiscing elit. Mauris ornare odio vel risus. Maecenas elit metus, pellentesque quis, pretium.

Next   Cancel

If you have more than one monitor, you can apply different **ClearType** settings to each monitor.

4 Choose the setting that's best for you, click **Next** and then **Finish**

System Information
has an expandable
category list on the
left that leads to more
specific detail of the
system's hardware and
software. It will also
give you details about
any devices that are not
working properly.

Don't forget

Device Manager
is a very useful
troubleshooting tool. If a
device is flagged with a
warning symbol, double-
clicking it opens a dialog
box that will tell you the
nature of the problem,
plus a suggested course
of action.

System Details

Windows provides two useful tools for users who need to get
details about their system.

System Information
The first is the **System Information** utility. This gives detailed
information about all the hardware and software on the PC.
To open it, go to the Taskbar **Search** box and type "msinfo32.exe".
The main page gives a System Summary that details items such as
the CPU, the amount of installed memory, operating system, etc.

Device Manager
This utility allows you to view,
configure, and troubleshoot your
PC's hardware devices. To open it,
go to the Taskbar **Search** box and
type "devmgr.msc".

Device Manager lists all your
system's hardware. Expanding the
categories gives details, and access
to the system properties, for the
individual devices.

Device Manager also flags any
devices that are not working with
warning symbols, and allows you to
install and update device drivers.

...cont'd

Third-Party Utilities

While **System Information** and the **Device Manager** provide a lot of information about the system, there are many third-party utilities that provide greater detail. One of the best is **SiSoft Sandra** (shown below) – available for download at **sisoftware.net** For really in-depth details about your system, it is a highly-recommended download.

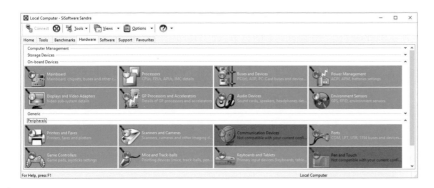

Video and Audio Codecs

A problem some users encounter when trying to play a video file is that they get sound but no video (or no sound in the case of a sound file). The reason is that the file's codec (see the Don't forget tip) is missing. To resolve the issue, you need to download and install it. The difficulty is knowing which codec is needed. Go to **headbands.com/gspot** and download a program called **GSpot**. Open the errant file with **GSpot** and you will be told which codec it was compressed with, and lots of other information about the file, then do a web search for the required codec.

SiSoft Sandra is available in various versions. The **Lite** version, which is free, will give you all the information you need.

Another good utility is the **Belarc Advisor**. This is available for free download at **belarc.com**

201

A codec is a program that compresses the data in sound and video files, thus reducing the size of the files. When the file is played, the same codec must be installed on the PC in order to decompress it.

Online Data Storage

In the previous edition of this book, we wrote about the plethora of websites offering online data storage facilities. Some were offering limited amounts (typically 2-5GB) for free, while larger amounts were available for a fee.

With Windows 10, Microsoft has jumped on this bandwagon by providing an app called **OneDrive** (previously called SkyDrive). This is available from the Start menu and gives users 5GB of online storage (correct at the time of printing).

To get started, click the **OneDrive** tile and log on with your Microsoft Account. If you don't have an account, you will need to create one. Once done, you will see the following:

A **OneDrive** account can be accessed in two ways: directly from a web browser or via the Windows 10 **OneDrive** app that places a **OneDrive** icon in **File Explorer**. More options are available to you when it is accessed via a web browser online.

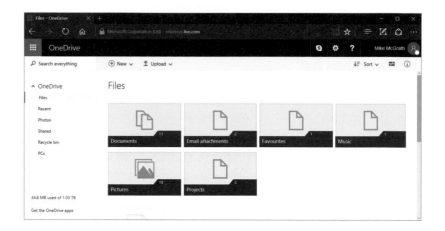

OneDrive starts you off with a number of folders as shown above. You can create more, and also nest folders within folders. To upload and download data, click a folder to open it and then right-click to open an options bar at the bottom of the screen. This provides the relevant commands.

A really cool feature of **OneDrive** is that it is available as a **Save** option from the file menus of many other apps and programs, such as Microsoft Office 2016.

Features of **OneDrive** include: easy drag-and-drop uploading and downloading, global access to your data, and the convenience of Windows' **File Explorer** to manage your files and folders.

OneDrive does much more than just provide a place to store data. By integrating it with a Microsoft Account, it can be used to synchronize files, photos, video, email, documents, etc. across a number of separate devices, such as PCs, smartphones and tablets.

Problem Steps Recorder

As the local PC guru, you're probably resigned to friends and family pestering you for help with their computer problems. This is bad enough, but when they are unable to clearly explain what the problem is or what they've done, as is often the case, it becomes very difficult, or even impossible, to help them.

A little known utility supplied with Windows 10 may provide the answer. When you get one of these irritating phone calls, tell the caller to go to their PC, type "psr" into the Taskbar **Search** box and press **Enter**. This will open Windows 10's **Steps Recorder**.

Once they have this running, get them to press **Start Record**, and reproduce the fault or do whatever it was they did, again. **Steps Recorder** will capture every mouse click and keystroke. When they've finished, they press **Stop Record** and a report is generated and saved as a **ZIP** file. This can then be emailed to you. When you open the report, you will see a detailed step-by-step list of every action that was made. Even more helpful is the fact that screenshots are included, as shown below:

You must run Problem Steps Recorder as an administrator in elevated mode to record any activities that need administrator authority.

Some programs, for example a full screen game, might not be captured accurately or provide useful details.

This is useful for the reverse situation as well – trying to explain how to do something to the user. A series of screenshots indicating where to click will be much easier for an inexperienced user to follow.

Easy Device Management

A useful feature of Windows 10 is **Device Stage**, the purpose of which is to simplify user interaction with devices such as cell phones, printers, MP3 players, digital cameras, etc. Basically, it provides a one-stop solution for managing all tasks related to the device in question. It works as follows:

1 Go to **Control Panel** > **Devices and Printers**. You will see a set of high-resolution icons for all the devices connected to your PC:

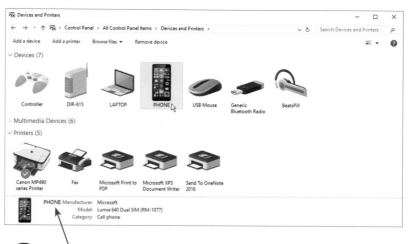

2 Details of a selected device are presented at the bottom of the window when you click a device icon. Double-click a device icon and a new window will open, from where you can access settings for the device and its features. This is the **Device Stage**. In the example below, we see options for this system's default Canon printer. The options available vary according to the type of device.

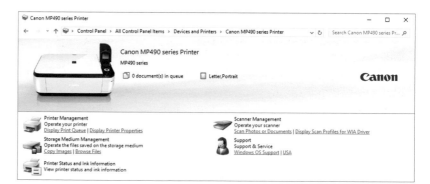

Hot tip

Not all devices work with **Device Stage**. Support for the feature must be built in to the device by the manufacturer.

Hot tip

You are also presented with options when you connect a device if you click the notification box:

Reset Your Computer

We saw on page 125 that the traditional method of completely restoring a Windows PC to its factory settings is to do a clean installation. This wipes the drive clean of all data, after which a new copy of Windows is installed. This is done by booting the PC from the installation disk – a procedure that most users will be wary of trying.

Windows 10 provides a much simpler method of restoring Windows to its factory settings. This is courtesy of its **Reset** utility. It works as described below:

 Go to **Settings** > **Update & security** > **Recovery**. Under "Reset this PC", click **Get started**

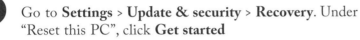 You will be presented with the two options shown below:

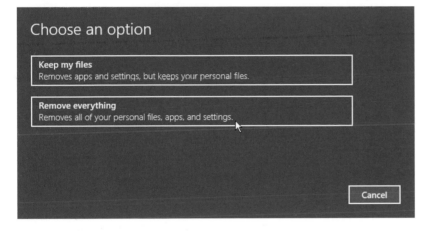

Choose an option

Keep my files
Removes apps and settings, but keeps your personal files.

Remove everything
Removes all of your personal files, apps, and settings.

Cancel

Choose the first, **Keep my files**, if you just want to restore your PC with an "as new" copy of Windows, but keep your stuff.

Choose the second, **Remove everything**, if you want to start again from scratch with an "as new" PC. You will then be given the choice of **Just remove my files** or **Remove my files and clean the drive**. The first option here is quicker, but the second option is more secure – usually done when a PC is being sold or scrapped.

 Select the required option and then sit back as Windows is restored

The **Reset** utility provides an ideal way to securely deleting your data on a computer you are going to sell or scrap.

Remember to back up your personal data before performing a **Reset** unless you choose to **Keep my files**.

The **Reset** process will require you to enter certain information, such as your location and your Wi-Fi key – just like installing Windows 10 for the very first time.

PC Recovery Options

Windows 10 is a very stable and reliable operating system. However, it will inevitably go wrong on occasion and so users need to be aware of steps they can take to resolve any issues they experience.

If the problem is not too serious and the user can still get into Windows, the procedure is as follows:

You can safely explore the **Advanced startup** options described here, then press the on-screen ⬅ back button to return to the first screen and choose **Continue**, to exit to Windows as normal.

1 Go to **Settings** > **Update & security** > **Recovery**. Under **Advanced startup**, click **Restart now**

2 When the system restarts, choose **Troubleshoot** to see the following screen:

3 The **Reset your PC** option was described on the previous page. Click **Advanced options** to see a list of other troubleshooting options:

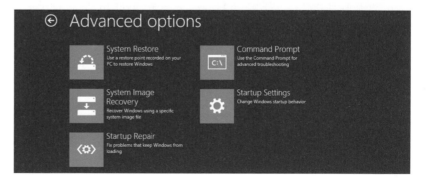

If your PC simply will not boot up properly try the **Startup Repair** option before anything else – it may well fix the problem. See **Startup Settings** on page 207.

System Restore enables the PC to be restored to the state it was in when the restore point was made. This is ideal for resolving minor issues – see page 208.

System Image Recovery is similar to System Restore as it restores the PC from an image file to a previous state, but unlike System Restore it destroys all the user's data. Accordingly, it is a "last resort" option to be used only when all others have failed.

Startup Repair attempts to resolve issues that are preventing the PC from starting. So if your PC won't boot up, this is the option to try first. See **Startup Settings** below.

Command Prompt is for advanced users only. It appears before Windows loads and can be used to enter commands to diagnose, check components, and other recovery options.

Startup Settings provides a list of further troubleshooting options, such as Safe Mode, Low-Resolution Video Mode, Boot Logging and more.

If the problem is so serious that you cannot get Windows running at all, you will have to access the recovery options a different way.

If you have a Windows 10 installation disk, the recovery options will be available from this. Configure the PC to boot from the CD/DVD drive as described on page 125, place the installation disk in the drive and then boot the PC. When the **Install now** screen opens, you will see a **Repair your computer** option at the bottom. Click this and the recovery options will open. If you don't have an installation disk – as many PCs these days are sold without one – you will have to create a recovery disk. Windows provides you with an option to do this. However, you need to do it while your PC is functional – it's no good waiting until it has failed. You can do it by going to the **Control Panel** and clicking **Recovery**. Select the first option **Create a recovery drive** and simply follow the prompts. Note that you will need a USB drive for this.

If you want to start your PC in **Safe Mode**, select **Startup Settings** then click the **Restart** button that appears and choose the **F4** key option.

In Windows 10, **Safe Mode** cannot be initiated with the **F8** key as it could with previous versions of Windows.

If you don't have a Windows 10 installation disk, be sure to create a recovery drive – you might need it one day!

207

```
Recovery                                                    —   □   ×
←  →  ∨  ↑  🗖 > Control Panel > All Control Panel Items > Recovery    ∨  Ɔ   Search Control Panel   ρ
                                                                                        ❓
Control Panel Home          Advanced recovery tools

                            💽 Create a recovery drive
                            Create a recovery drive to troubleshoot problems when your PC can't start.

                            💽 Open System Restore
                            Undo recent system changes, but leave files such as documents, pictures, and music unchanged.

                            💽 Configure System Restore
                            Change restore settings, manage disk space, and create or delete restore points.
See also
File History                If you're having problems with your PC, go to Settings and try resetting it
```

System Restore

When a computer is new, it is fast and responsive and everything works as it should. Fast-forward a few months and it will already have begun to slow down and develop minor but probably irritating problems.

Very few users have the technical knowledge to be able to resolve Windows faults, so Windows includes a utility known as **System Restore**. This can be used to create a restore point that is basically a snapshot, or image, of the PC at a given point.

Should the PC subsequently develop a fault that the user cannot fix, the PC can be restored from the restore point:

1 Open **System Restore** as described on page 206

System Restore   ×

Restore your computer to the state it was in before the selected event

Current time zone: FLE Daylight Time

Date and Time	Description	Type
8/22/2016 6:03:56 AM	WLSetup	Install
8/19/2016 11:38:58 AM	Windows Update	Critical Update
8/15/2016 10:19:57 AM	Installed Adobe Photoshop CS2	Install
8/13/2016 3:57:04 PM	Windows Update	Critical Update

☑ Show more restore points   Scan for affected programs

                                        < Back   Next >   Cancel

2 Check the **Show more restore points** box to display a list of all available restore points

3 Choose a restore point made at a time prior to the fault manifesting itself. Click **Next**, and the utility will restore your system from the restore point selected

Beware

System Restore points can occupy several gigabytes of disk space. If you find yourself running low, consider deleting some of them as explained on page 31.

Hot tip

Configuration options for **System Restore** can be found by going to **Control Panel** > **System** > **System Protection**.

Install Java

Java is a modern technology that is used in a multitude of applications, e.g. utilities, games and business applications. It is found on millions of computers around the world, and on billions of devices, such as smartphones, tablets, games consoles and TVs.

Java is also used extensively on websites and, without it, many of the web applications that users take for granted just won't work. Typical examples are online games, calendars, calculators, etc. It's also integral to the intranet applications and e-business solutions that are the basis of computing in the corporate world.

Java is not included with Windows 10, however, nor is it currently supported by the Microsoft Edge web browser.

Users who require Java support must use the Internet Explorer browser included with Windows 10 and install the Java plugin themselves. Java is free and can be downloaded from **java.com**

Some Java applications, such as animated 3D online games, require a lot of system resources, and so users with under-powered computers may find it beneficial to turn Java off when browsing certain sites. This can be done by clicking the Tools icon at the top-right of Internet Explorer and then clicking **Manage add-ons**. Find the Java entry, right-click and select **Disable**.

Java provides a platform for the development of applications that work on multiple operating systems. Essentially, that means a program written in Java will run on any type of computing platform.

If your browser is not Java-enabled, when you visit a site that uses Java you will just see a blank space where the Java applet is positioned.

Be On Time with Windows

The timekeeping utility provided with Windows 10 has two cool features that many users will find useful.

Additional clocks
The first one enables you to have up to three clocks all set to different time zones:

 1 Go to **Control Panel > Date and Time**, then choose the **Additional Clocks** tab

 2 Check **Show this clock**, then select a time zone and enter an appropriate display name for each extra clock

 3 Next, hover the pointer over the system clock to see all the clocks

Tuesday, August 23, 2016

Tue 9:30 AM (Local time)
Tue 2:30 AM (New York)
Mon 11:30 PM (Los Angeles)

 4 Now, click the system clock to see a larger view displaying all your clocks with their current time, plus the calendar view

Reset the clock accurately
The usual method of resetting the PC's clock involves clicking little arrows, which is fiddly. There's also no guarantee that your reference clock is accurate. Windows provides an easier way that is also extremely accurate:

Repeat Step 1 above and then click the **Internet Time** tab. Click **Change settings** and from the drop-down box, select a time server. Then, click the **Update now** button.

Hot tip

You can also access the **Date and time** dialog via **Settings** > **Time & language** > **Data and time** > **Add clocks for different time zones**.

Hot tip

All of the time servers used by the **Windows Time** utility are synchronized with atomic clocks to guarantee accuracy.

210

Internet Time Settings

Configure Internet time settings:

☑ Synchronize with an Internet time server

Server: time.windows.com   Update now

The clock was successfully synchronized with time.windows.com on 8/23/2016 at 9:34 AM.

OK   Cancel

Index

213

Liked this book? More titles to stay ahead in easy steps

Why choose this book?

It's written in plain English
Put off by the jargon? Don't worry, we keep things straightforward.

It's easy to follow
Clear, step-by-step instructions make learning simple.

It's fully illustrated
We don't just tell you how to do it, we also **show** you how.

It's in full color
This book's printed in color to make it simpler to use and easier on the eye.

And it's fantastic value
Do we need to say any more?

£10.99 UK / $14.99 US

ISBN 978-1-84078-748-1   US$14.99
5 1 4 9 9 >
9 781840 787481

Oh, so that's how you do it! Over a thousand useful tricks of the trade to make Windows work more efficiently for you – all revealed here. **Windows 10 Tips, Tricks & Shortcuts in easy steps,** now in its second edition, will teach how to:

- Customize the interface to suit your needs
- Boost your PC's performance with simple tweaks
- Quicken Startup and Shut down times
- Save time by keeping your files organized
- Keep your hard drive lean
- Quickly repair Windows 10
- Give your PC a free tune-up
- Keep net browsing safe, private and efficient
- Keep tabs on other users' activities
- Guard your PC against viruses and prying eyes
- Use a PC to build a home entertainment center

With keyboard shortcuts throughout to help you save time, this popular guide is a great investment for all Windows 10 users!

Let these icons make it even easier

 to spice up your learning

 highlights something worth remembering

 wards you off potential danger!

 indicates a new or changed feature

Categories: Computers/Microsoft Windows

www.ineasysteps.com